PROJECT

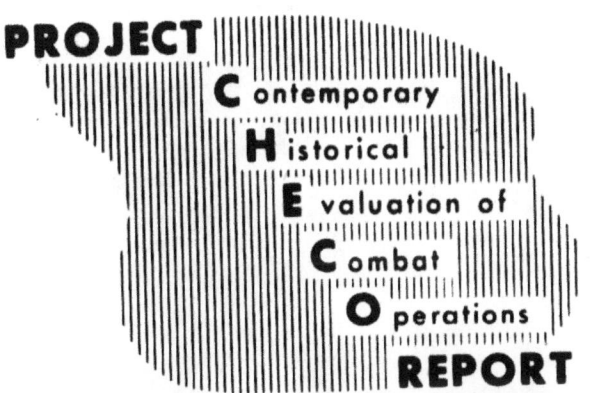

Contemporary
Historical
Evaluation of
Combat
Operations

REPORT

KHE SANH

(OPERATION NIAGARA)

22 JANUARY - 31 MARCH 68

13 SEPTEMBER 1968

HQ PACAF

Directorate, Tactical Evaluation
CHECO Division

Prepared by:

Mr. Warren A. Trest

Project CHECO 7th AF, DOAC

DOTEC-68-50

K717.0413-35

REPLY TO
ATTN OF: DOTEC   8 October 1968

SUBJECT: Change to Project CHECO Report, "Khe Sanh (Operation NIAGARA) 22 January-31 March 1968"

TO: All Holders of Subject Report

It is requested that holders of subject report, (S) 13 September 1968, DOTEC-68-50 remove page 49-50 and insert the attached revised pages.

FOR THE COMMANDER IN CHIEF

WARREN H. PETERSON, Colonel, USAF   1 Atch
Chief, CHECO Division   Revised Pages 49-50 (C)
Directorate, Tactical Evaluation
DCS/Operations

This letter does not contain classified
information and may be declassified if
attachment is removed from it.

REPLY TO
ATTN OF: DOTEC   13 September 1968

SUBJECT: Project CHECO Report, "Khe Sanh (Operation NIAGARA), 22 January-
          31 March 1968"

TO: SEE DISTRIBUTION PAGE

1. Attached is a SECRET NOFORN document. It shall be transported, stored, safeguarded, and accounted for in accordance with applicable security directives. Each page is marked according to its contents. SPECIAL HANDLING REQUIRED, NOT RELEASABLE TO FOREIGN NATIONALS. The information contained in this document will not be disclosed to foreign nationals or their representatives. Retain or destroy in accordance with AFR 205-1. Do not return.

2. This letter does not contain classified information and may be declassified if attachment is removed from it.

FOR THE COMMANDER IN CHIEF

WARREN H. PETERSON, Colonel, USAF   1 Atch
Chief, CHECO Division   Proj CHECO Rpt (SNF),
Directorate, Tactical Evaluation   13 Sep 68
DCS/Operations

DISTRIBUTION

HQ USAF

AFAAC	1 Cy
AFAMA	1 Cy
AFBSA	1 Cy
AFCCS-SA	1 Cy
AFCHO	2 Cys
AFGOA	2 Cys
AFIIN	1 Cy
AFISI	3 Cys
AFISL	1 Cy
AFMSG	1 Cy
AFNINA	1 Cy
AFNINCC	1 Cy
AFNINDE	3 Cys
AFOAPS	1 Cy
AFOCC	1 Cy
AFOCE	1 Cy
AFOMO	1 Cy
AFOWX	1 Cy
AFPDP	1 Cy
AFPMRE	1 Cy
AFRDC	1 Cy
AFRDR	1 Cy
AFRDQ	1 Cy
AFSLP	1 Cy
AFSMS	1 Cy
AFSME	1 Cy
AFSSS	1 Cy
AFSTP	1 Cy
AFXOP	1 Cy
AFXOPS	1 Cy
AFXOSL	1 Cy
AFXOSO	1 Cy
AFXOSN	1 Cy
AFXOPR	1 Cy
AFXOTZ	1 Cy
AFXPD	9 Cys
AFXDOC	1 Cy
AFXDOD	1 Cy
AFXDOL	1 Cy

SAFOI	2 Cys
SAFLL	1 Cy
SAFAA	1 Cy

MAJCOM

AU (ASI-HA)	2 Cys
AU (ASI-ASAD)	1 Cy
AU (AUL3T-66-7)	1 Cy
AU (ACSC)	1 Cy
ADC (ADODC)	1 Cy
ADC (ADOOP)	2 Cys
ADC (ADLPP)	2 Cys
TAC (DO-O)	1 Cy
TAC (DPL)	2 Cys
TAC (DOTS)	1 Cy
TAC (DORQ)	1 Cy
TAC (DI)	1 Cy
MAC (MAFOI)	1 Cy
MAC (MAOID)	1 Cy
MAC (MAOCO)	1 Cy
AFSC (SCL)	8 Cys
AFSC (SCO)	2 Cys
AFLC (MCO)	1 Cy
AFLC (MCF)	1 Cy
ATC (ATXDC)	1 Cy
SAC (DO)	1 Cy
SAC (DPL)	1 Cy
SAC (DXI)	1 Cy
SAC (DIX)	1 Cy
SAC (OA)	1 Cy
USAFA (OI)	1 Cy
USAFA (DFH)	1 Cy
USAFE (OPL)	2 Cys
USAFSO (BIOH)	1 Cy
USAFSS (ODC)	1 Cy
USAFSS (COI-5)	1 Cy

OTHERS

9AF (DO)	1 Cy
12AF (DI)	1 Cy
19AF (DA-C)	1 Cy
USAFAGOS	1 Cy
USAFSAWC (DO)	1 Cy
USAFTAWC (DA)	1 Cy
USAFTARC (DI)	1 Cy
USAFTALC (DA)	1 Cy
USAFTFWC (CRCD)	1 Cy
FTD (TDPI)	1 Cy
AFAITC	1 Cy
SRAFREP (SWC)	1 Cy

PACAF

DP	1 Cy
DI	1 Cy
DO	1 Cy
DPL	1 Cy
DXIH	1 Cy
5AF (DOP)	1 Cy
7AF (DOAC)	9 Cys
13AF (DOP)	1 Cy
13AF (DXI)	1 Cy
834AIRDIV	1 Cy
3TFW	1 Cy
8TFW	1 Cy
12TFW	1 Cy
14SOW	1 Cy
31TFW	1 Cy
35TFW	1 Cy
37TFW	1 Cy
56ACW	1 Cy
315ACW	1 Cy
355TFW	1 Cy
366TFW	1 Cy
388TFW	1 Cy
432TRW	1 Cy
460TRW	1 Cy
483TAW	1 Cy
553RECON WG	1 Cy
6400 TEST SQ	1 Cy
DOTEC	6 Cys

TABLE OF CONTENTS

	Page
Introduction	1
The Tactical Situation	2
7th Air Force Planning	6
The Fall of "Elephant"	13
NIAGARA and the Tet Offensive	20
The Fall of Lang Vei	29
Attack Against Hill 861	43
Targeting and Tactical Response	45
ARC LIGHT Responsiveness	66
Enemy Counter Air Activities	71
Tactical Airlift at Khe Sanh	73
Coordination and Control	77
Operations Summary	87
Epilogue	96
FOOTNOTES	101

APPENDIXES

I.	NIAGARA Daily Sorties	112
II.	Reconnaissance Objectives	115
III.	Tactical Air Cumulative BDA	118
IV.	Photo Significant Items	123
V.	Total Ordnance Expended by 7th Air Force	124
VI.	Khe Sanh Airlift Summary	125

GLOSSARY 130

FIGURES	Follows Page
1	6
2	10
3	34
4	34
5	44
6	48
7	48
8	48
9	52
10	52
11	52
12	58
13	70
14	74
15	74
16	74
17	78

OPERATION NIAGARA

Introduction

Operation NIAGARA was a concentrated air effort executed by the 7th Air Force Commander in early 1968 to disrupt a potential major offensive in northwestern I Corps and the contiguous area of Laos. An extensive enemy build-up in the western DMZ area in late 1967 and early 1968 indicated that a major offensive was developing, with the estimated objective of overrunning Khe Sanh and other friendly positions located astride Route 9--the most readily accessible infiltration route for North Vietnamese forces bypassing the DMZ into South Vietnam. It was further estimated that the enemy would launch his offensive on or about 30 January--when the South Vietnamese would be observing the Lunar New Year. Thus, at the direction of COMUSMACV, the 7th Air Force Commander and his operations and intelligence staff planned and directed SLAM-type operations in the NIAGARA area several days prior to the Tet Holidays. These operations were accorded the highest priority, and were applied on a sustained basis. [1]

SLAM-type operations began in the NIAGARA area on 22 January, with 595 tactical strike sorties (including 7AF, USMC, and USN) and 49 B-52 sorties flown against enemy targets. When Operation NIAGARA officially terminated on 31 March 1968, over 24,400 tactical strike sorties and 2,500 B-52 sorties had been flown. This was the greatest sustained concentration of airpower in the Vietnam conflict to date. The purpose of this report is to bring the statistical weight of effort into proper perspective through the narrative study and documentation of significant developments. It addresses in particular those operational areas of 7th Air Force evaluative concern--i.e. operational problems and lessons learned, coordination and control, the development of targets and tactics, and the responsiveness of airpower to the tactical situation. 2/

During the progress of NIAGARA operations, COMUSMACV designated the Deputy Commander for Air Operations as the single manager for control of tactical air resources (strike and reconnaissance) throughout South Vietnam and the extended battle area. The Deputy Commander for Air was specifically charged with the responsibility for coordinating and directing the tactical air effort. Although Operation NIAGARA precipitated the single management directive, the intricacies of this subject deserve more in-depth treatment. A separate Project CHECO study, "Single Manager for Air in SVN," addresses the single manager concept for control of tactical air resources as applied in South Vietnam and the extended battle area. Only those specific problems resulting from divided control in the NIAGARA area are discussed in this text.

The Tactical Situation

A fair assessment of the developing situation was that the enemy, within his available resources, had been temporarily stalemated by aggressive joint air/ground operations, and that he would now make a major attempt to reverse this tactical situation. This attempt would require a greatly increased infiltration effort. Thus, while promoting increased talk of negotiations on the international front, the enemy had used monsoon cover and the Christmas truce to accelerate his infiltration of men and materiel to the southern assembly areas, which included Cambodia. The stage for widespread offensives in South Vietnam and Laos was being set.

A comparison of truck sightings in the infiltration corridors clearly shows the quantum surge in the enemy's infiltration capability to support the upcoming offensive. As an example: for the first nine months of 1967, there was a monthly average of 480 truck sightings. Sightings surged to 1,116 in October, 3,823 in November, and 6,315 in December; this is in sharp contrast to the monthly average of 256 sightings during the last three months of 1966. Although there had been a major improvement in 7AF capabilities for truck detection, the surge was still evident. [3] Friendly ground forces were engaged in small-scale operations throughout the country. COMUSMACV advised his staff in early January that "the enemy has completely shifted his strategy". He reported that enemy forces had moved from the defense to the offense, and were "on the move everywhere". [4]

Although enemy activity was on the rise throughout the southern infiltration corridors and tactical zones, the greatest threat appeared to be in the III Marine Amphibious Forces (MAF) tactical area of responsibility (TAOR) in northern I Corps. Over the past several months, the Marine TAOR had closed northward, and fixed positions had been established across the northern portion of I Corps to effect a barrier below the DMZ. Also, several large scale ground operations had been executed by III MAF to counter the growing threat throughout the northern provinces, and U.S. Army and ARVN ground units had moved northward to strengthen the Allied posture. As the threat grew, further augmentation of the Marine ground capability became necessary, as did the application of increased B-52 and tactical airstrikes in support of the critical ground situation.

A prelude to Operation NIAGARA was III MAF's Operation SCOTLAND, which had been conducted since November 1967 to counter the growing threat to Khe Sanh, Camp Carroll, Quang Tri City, and other positions in northwestern I Corps. During mid-January, the undeniable threat in the Khe Sanh area prompted the greatest concern. Not only had the enemy positioned a large number of forces around Khe Sanh, but intelligence sources reported that Routes 92 and 9 in Laos showed signs of an increased logistical movement into this area--indicating a pivot point for operations leading toward Khe Sanh. [5]

To exploit this situation, COMUSMACV ordered an all source intelligence effort directed by MACV J-2 to develop target boxes for B-52 strikes. A maximum B-52 effort was applied against targets generated by this program. Known as NIAGARA I, this effort was executed in mid-January. Planning for SLAM-type operations around the Khe Sanh area (NIAGARA II) envisioned the employment of all available USN, USMC and USAF strike, reconnaissance, and electronic warfare aircraft resources as required. Lower scales of activity were contemplated consistent with threat levels. [6]

In planning for NIAGARA, COMUSMACV advised the CG, III MAF on 6 January 1968: [7]

> *"The anticipated build-up of enemy forces in the western DMZ area provides an opportunity to plan a comprehensive intelligence collection effort and to make preparations for coordinated B-52 and*

> *tactical airstrikes. We should be prepared to surprise and disrupt enemy plans for an offensive against Khe Sanh with heavy bombing attacks on a sustained basis."*

Following a meeting with COMUSMACV on the tactical situation, the 7th Air Force Commander advised his operations and intelligence staff on 9 January that a major enemy offensive within the next few weeks was deemed a certainty. He cautioned, however, that the offensive could be directed against targets throughout South Vietnam. His memorandum of 9 January advised: [8]

> *"The enemy now has the better part of the 325th, 304th and 320th Divisions in the vicinity of Khe Sanh. From the disposition of these forces, it would appear that Khe Sanh is the intended target. However, there is no hard evidence to support this course of action as the enemy's intention. The build-up of forces and materiel seems to indicate a much broader objective than Khe Sanh. He may be in the midst of a major build-up to wrest the initiative from us throughout the country. All of the talks of negotiation may be a trap to get the bombing stopped so as to accelerate the delivery of more equipment into SVN with the objective of a military victory in 1968. He may be after much bigger game than Khe Sanh."*

The Commander cautioned his staff that action in all four Corps Tactical Zones (CTZ) was on the upswing. There were no large unit fights at the time, but there was a significant increase in small unit actions. He advised: [9]

> *"It is expected this trend will continue. MACV thinks the number of enemy actions is at an all time high since 1965--certainly higher than at any time in my tour. All of these small unit fights seem to tie together a general strategy of offensive actions at all levels throughout the country. Many of the attacks are directed against local leaders. The obvious aim is to tighten control on the local people. His fight has always kept the objective of controlling the people uppermost."*

This would prove to be a sound assessment of the developing situation when the enemy launched his Lunar New Year offensive a few weeks later. In the meanwhile, the disposition of enemy forces in the NIAGARA area represented a very real threat to the Marines at Khe Sanh, while also presenting "an undeniable opportunity for concentrated airstrikes on a sustained basis." Mounting enemy infiltration, coupled with intelligence estimates that Tet was the key date in enemy planning, prompted a strong sense of urgency concerning the defense of Khe Sanh. The 7AF Commander directed his staff to assemble a planning team for NIAGARA. "I want to emphasize the urgency of the plan," he stated, "You have authority to draw on whatever staff assistance is needed. Marines must be brought in as the plan develops. It must be our best effort to support their defenses at Khe Sanh." 10/

7th Air Force Planning

COMUSMACV advised that he considered it imperative that "maximum air firepower available" be used to meet the enemy threat in I Corps. He also emphasized the requirement to "effect detailed application of air resources in I Corps," which would require a more centralized direction of the air effort in the threat area. To this end, he defined the command and control procedures which would apply in NIAGARA operations: 11/

> "To meet the threat in the Quang Tri - Thua Thien area, I have directed my Deputy Comdr MACV Air, Gen Momyer, to develop a plan to concentrate all available air resources (SLAM-type Operation). The direct support of Marine units by the 1st MAW is not affected by this plan. The initial area of concentration will be around the Khe Sanh (NIAGARA II) area. Depending upon the tactical situation the area will be shifted. Dep COMUSMACV for Air Operations will coordinate the details of this air

6

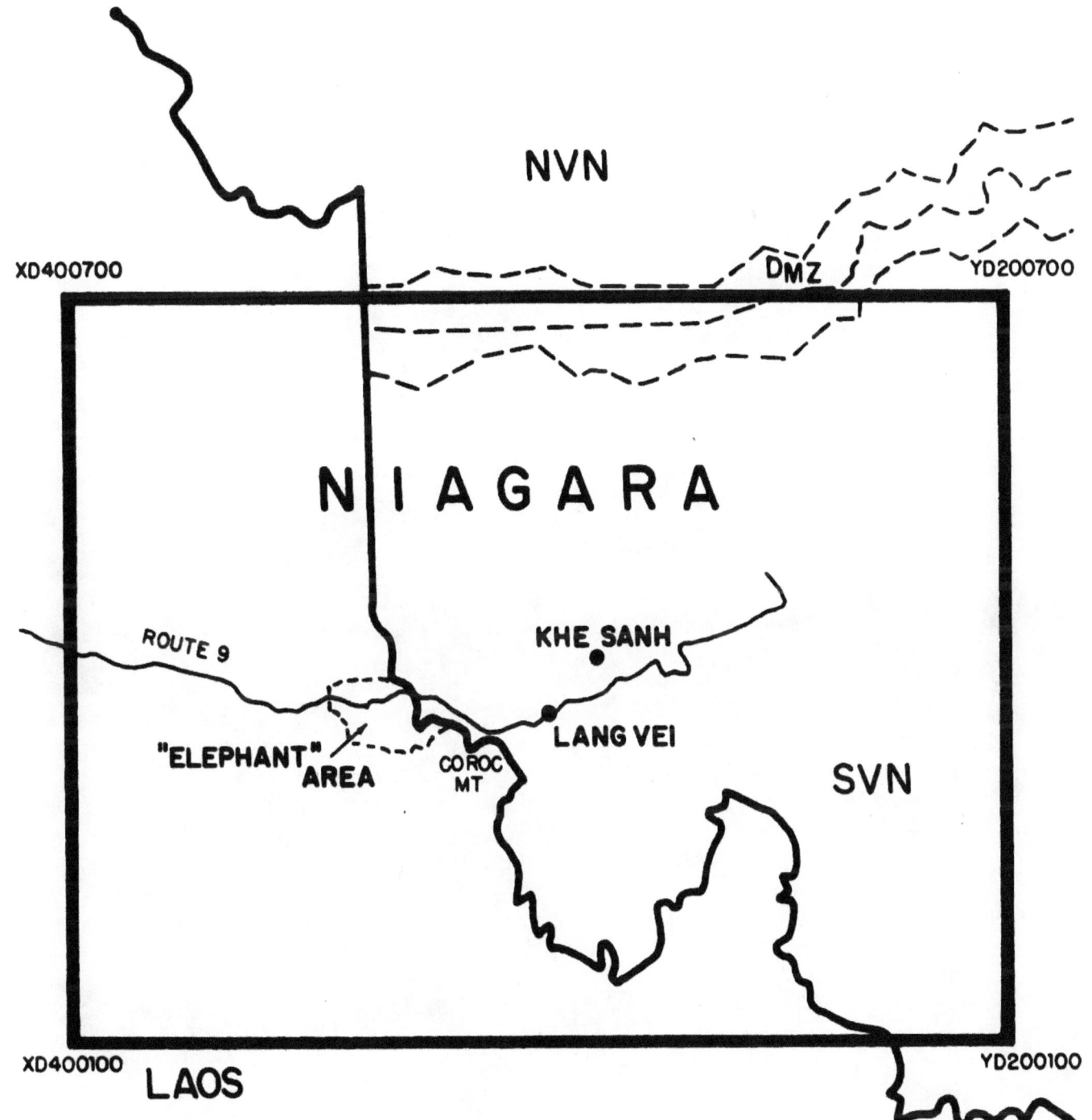

FIGURE 1

> *plan with the 1st Marine Air Wing and III MAF as appropriate. I have charged him with the overall responsibility for air operations for the execution of this plan. He will coordinate and direct the employment of the tactical air, Marine air, diverted airstrikes from out of country air operations, and such naval air that may be requested. B-52 strikes will be coordinated through him.*
>
> *"Until further notice, it is directed that III MAF make available to 7AF all tactical bomber sorties not required for direct air support of Marine units. These sorties will be initially committed to the NIAGARA operation.*
>
> *"I wish to stress the absolute necessity for coordination of all elements of the command to bring our firepower against the enemy in the most effective manner. The serious threat we face in I Corps and Khe Sanh in particular, demands this. I have directed my Air Deputy to insure in my name that these air resources are applied to this end."*

To insure that adequate air resources and tactical flexibility were available to the 7AF Commander, COMUSMACV requested authority from CINCPAC to divert as much of the air effort committed to ROLLING THUNDER "as may be considered necessary to counter the enemy build-up in Quang Tri Province". This included both Thailand based USAF aircraft and Seventh Fleet resources. [12/] CINCPAC concurred, but advised that "it is essential" that interdiction efforts in Route Package I and Laos be continued. [13/] This authority for Thai-based aircraft to conduct strikes against targets in I Corps marked the first use of Thai-based aircraft in South Vietnam (SVN). The rules of engagement had previously restricted use of these aircraft to strikes in Laos and North Vietnam (NVN).

From the outset of NIAGARA planning, the 7AF Commander directed his staff to make a major effort to insure that effective coordination between participating forces was accomplished. He further directed that the air effort be geared to the overall defense plan for the tactical area. 14/ As advised in a message to III MAF on 19 January: 15/

> *"Deputy COMUSMACV for Air is preparing an outline plan to insure that all elements of air planning for support of Operation NIAGARA are complete and that command, control, and coordination arrangements among forces involved are adequate to the full scale of intensity of possible air operations."*

Specific planning for operations as approved by COMUSMACV in NIAGARA II called for a maximum B-52 effort, with follow-up reconnaissance--both visual and photo. Tactical air would expend under FAC control. Airborne Command and Control Center (ABCCC) aircraft orbiting over Laos would control the SLAM effort. The ABCCC would serve as an extension to the 7AF Tactical Air Control Center (TACC), and would be tied into the Marines at Khe Sanh and Dong Ha for artillery fire. Intensified armed reconnaissance into and leading out of the NIAGARA area would be required, and all roads leading from Laos into the area were to be interdicted. The 7AF Commander also directed that SLAM surveillance and suppression were to be available if required, and that Air Defense CAP be prepared to screen off offensive air that might covertly develop. He also directed on the spot analysis at the TACC for indications of enemy attempts to put an airfield into operation in Laos and Route Package I. Detailed photo coverage would be directed for both day and night. 16/

TACC directed the "Covey" FACs flying out of Da Nang and Ubon Air Bases to place first priority on support of Operation NIAGARA. The Marine ground forces would be given full ALO/FAC support whenever required. The I Corps VR program would also receive top priority. They advised the 20th Tactical Air Support Squadron (TASS) to "keep ahead of FAC and aircraft requirements and notify TACC of additional needs available". 17/ Hq 7AF TACC also directed that it was essential that "7AF FACs develop and report all suspect activities observed in the threat area." In addition to the Laotian portion of the threat area, "all routes and trail nets leading into the Khe Sanh area" would be covered extensively for troops and logistic support infiltrations. 18/ A special 7AF NIAGARA Intelligence Control Center was also established to effect an around the clock priority effort to insure the effective management of intelligence resources. This will be discussed later under "Targeting and Tactical Response".

Control and coordination limitations had been of recurring concern during joint air/ground operations in the III MAF TAOR. Thus, when COMUSMACV issued the execution order for NIAGARA II on 22 January, the 7AF Commander in turn directed his operations and intelligence staff to effect immediate coordination with III MAF officials. 7AF officials proceeded that afternoon to III MAF at Da Nang to brief and coordinate plans for air support of NIAGARA II. Present at the conference were the CG, III MAF, Comdr 1st MAW, the III MAF Chief of Staff, and several key III MAF staff officers. The 7AF Deputy Director, TACC, reported on this meeting: 19/

> "General Cushman (CG, III MAF) stated that he wanted all the air that he could get in support of his ground forces and that he preferred to use air to the maximum extent possible rather than artillery because of logistic resupply to the Khe Sanh area. General Cushman was concerned about Marine ground forces deployed in and around the Khe Sanh area and wanted to be sure that procedures were established to insure the safety of these troops. Also that the 155-mm artillery at Khe Sanh could be used, when necessary, under the control of the Fire Support Coordination Center (FSCC) at Khe Sanh. I informed General Cushman in my opinion this coordination was easily effected through the ABCCC and strikes made in the close proximity of Khe Sanh would be coordinated through that facility. In addition, if communications were lost at Khe Sanh I suggested that the Division FSCC at Dong Ha provide the necessary coordination.
>
> "Upon my departure from III MAF, I was convinced that General Cushman was delighted that 7th Air Force had taken the initiative and was providing air power to assist his ground forces. He further informed me that the only thing he asked was that strikes in the vicinity of his troops be thoroughly coordinated with his controlling agencies and that he preferred to use air rather than artillery because of the capability to deliver greater tonnage on the enemy."

It was agreed that the ABCCC would directly control all air operations in NIAGARA with the exception of those Marine sorties that were to be used for close air support of Marine ground forces. It was clearly understood that the procedures established would in no way restrict Hillsboro ABCCC from employing airpower in any area of NIAGARA, but certain coordination procedures would be required for the protection of friendly troops and effective use of artillery. For instance, a zone was established in the immediate vicinity of Khe Sanh where Marine troops were deployed that would require all strikes to be FAC controlled and with coordination through the FSCC. Outside of this zone, and out to a circle designating the 155-mm artillery range, strikes would be conducted after coordination with the Marine FSCC at Khe Sanh to

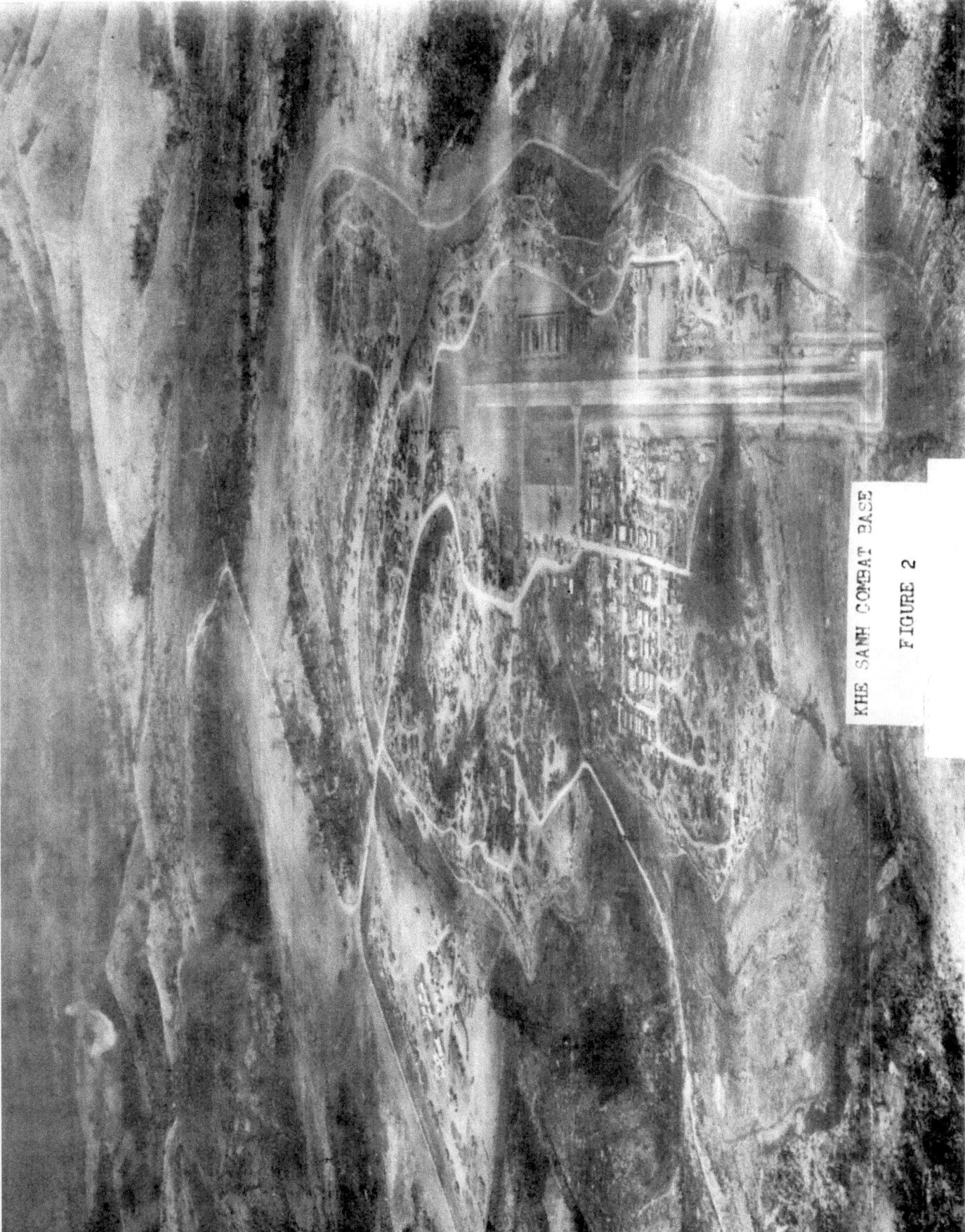

KHE SANH COMBAT BASE

FIGURE 2

insure that artillery and airstrikes did not interfere with each other. In other areas contiguous to the NIAGARA area, i.e. to the east through south, existing procedures would remain in effect. A free fire zone was established outside the 155-mm artillery range. Strikes could be made in this area without coordination of the FSCC. [20]

In specific areas designated by III MAF, in the immediate vicinity of Khe Sanh where Marine ground forces were deployed, Marine air would be used to the maximum extent possible. Additional strikes would be requested by the ground forces commander concerned. These strikes would be controlled either by FAC or MSQ/TPQ depending on the closeness of friendly troops. [21]

It was agreed that all aircraft operating in the NIAGARA area would check in and out with the ABCCC for target/FAC assignment with the exception of those Marine aircraft under FAC control conducting close air support of Marine ground forces in the immediate Khe Sanh area. The ABCCC would maintain coordination of these strikes through the Marine sub-DASC at Khe Sanh, or the airborne DASC if on station. When Marine aircraft were not used in this role they would contact the ABCCC to be put on other targets. [22]

With these agreements, the Deputy Director, TACC, departed Da Nang for Udorn to brief the ABCCC crews and to fly on Hillsboro ABCCC on 23 January to insure that these procedures were workable. He reported to the 7AF Commander: [23]

> *"While acting as the ABCCC Commander (Hillsboro) on the 23d I found that these procedures were effective and the operation went rather smoothly. The only problem*

> *encountered was initial coordination with the FSCC at Khe Sanh. ABCCC was unable to maintain radio contact with the FSCC. The orbit of ABCCC was moved in an attempt to gain constant radio contact; however, only intermittent contact was obtainable. Following this failure we established procedures to maintain constant radio contact with the Marine airborne DASC (really a TACP) that was on station between Da Nang and Khe Sanh. Once this procedure was established we had no more problems of coordinating strikes. For the first day I felt the operation went very well. However, procedures will continue to be refined and closer coordination attained.*
>
> *"Based on my experience on the 23d, I feel that the ABCCC can successfully handle 700 to 750 strike sorties in a 24 hour period so long as these sorties are not allowed to gang up at any one period. This situation can easily be prevented by proper scheduling and maintaining adequate tankers on station."*

Despite these early agreements, coordination and control problems did arise in NIAGARA, especially during the first three weeks. These problems, along with certain developments in this area of concern, are addressed under "Coordination and Control". Also, there was considerable coordination in other areas which are not addressed by this study. One example was coordination between COMUSMACV and the U.S. Ambassador to Laos on SLAM operations in the Laotian portion of the NIAGARA area. Ambassadorial concurrence was obtained, and prior approval on a large list of B-52 targets was given to insure no delay in the effective application of this weapons system. Along with other necessary restrictions, a no-fire zone was drawn around a friendly Laotian outpost just across the border on Route 9. This restriction was lifted shortly after NIAGARA operations began, when this outpost was overrun by NVN forces.

The Fall of "Elephant"

Several days prior to the beginning of NIAGARA, it was reported that the enemy had effectively restricted movement by friendly forces operating out of the Marine Base Camp at Khe Sanh and surrounding outposts. At this time, the III MAF had ten ground reconnaissance teams located at Khe Sanh. A MACV report advised that these teams had been able to accomplish "some ground reconnaissance", but had not produced "tangible" intelligence. Patrol range had been limited to an eight to ten kilometer radius of Khe Sanh because this was the limit of supporting fire available. Also, enemy counter reconnaissance patrols were able to screen the location and movement of units, and prevented the collection of data by engaging friendly patrols. 24/

By the time NIAGARA operations began, the situation had become more critical. Enemy forces had already begun sporadic but continuous shelling of the Khe Sanh Base Camp, and friendly outposts were effectively pinned down. Selected notes from the MACV Combat Operations Center log on 21-22 January tell the story: 25/

- At 210430 K/3/26 USMC on Hill 861 received a ground attack from an estimated 200-300 enemy. Friendly position was not penetrated and contact became sporadic until approximately 1200H when enemy broke contact. Sporadic small arms fire continued throughout the afternoon.

- At 210505H the Khe Sanh Combat Base received an unknown number of mortar rounds. Incoming mortar fire continued until 1200H. Evening of 21 January, the enemy began probing the perimeter wire defenses to the south and west of the airstrip. L/3/26 USMC repulsed the probe killing 25 enemy.

- Friendly casualty report for the day -- 14 KIA, 43 WIA.

- Three kilometers NNE of Khe Sanh at 211700H, three UH-1Ds in support of ARVN forces received heavy ground fire on approach to LZ. One UH-1D touched down in LZ, received heavy fire, and exploded. The other two UH-1Ds aborted mission and returned to Khe Sanh.

- On 22 January, both Khe Sanh and Hill 881 came under enemy mortar bombardment. Enemy positions taken under fire by tactical air and 105 fire.

- At 221300H, unknown number of civilians continue evacuating village of Khe Sanh to area near combat base.

- Approximately 1500H, an H-34 helicopter was shot down on Hill 881-S while on resupply mission. Vicinity Hill 861 an H-34 was shot down by enemy fire. Patrol located aircraft but could not locate crew.

- Twelve kilometers SSE of Khe Sanh at 221525H, an F-4B on CAS mission was hit by enemy ground fire and crashed.

- Eight kilometers NW of Khe Sanh at 221730H, I/3/26 USMC observed 30-40 enemy. Artillery missions and tactical air strikes directed on enemy positions. Results, 21 KIA.

- UPDATE. Twelve kilometers south of Khe Sanh at 211500H an air observer directed eight fixed wing strikes on enemy positions. Results, 40 KIA.

In the meanwhile, heavy enemy movement continued on the Laotian side of the NIAGARA area, and on the night of 23 January, an estimated three battalions of NVA soldiers attacked the Laotian outpost blocking Route 9 into South Vietnam.[26/] This friendly Laotian element, located at Ban Houi Sane, was officially known as BV-33, but was better known by its radio call sign -- "Elephant", especially to 7AF Covey FACs. These FACs were staging out of Khe Sanh prior to NIAGARA, but had been relocated to Da Nang and Ubon as the Khe Sanh situation became critical. The Elephant forces had proved to be a valuable intelligence source to the FACs, who not only maintained radio contact, but often flew into the camp's STOL strip for a visit with the BV-33 Commander,

Lt. Col. Soulang, and his people. [27]

As previously stated, 7th Air Force had gone to great lengths to preclude inadvertent strikes against the Elephant contingent, as well as other friendly positions on both sides of the border. A no-strike zone was drawn around the friendly positions, and the ABCCCs, the FACs, and all strike pilots were thoroughly briefed on these restricted areas. After 24 January, strike restrictions in the Elephant area were lifted--NVA forces had overrun the Elephant contingent. [28]

The attack on Elephant was supported by seven armored vehicles which had advanced along Route 9. [29] Weather was extremely bad in the area during the enemy advance, and this severely restricted air support for the Elephant forces. One Covey FAC described the weather: [30]

> *"On 24 January, I took off at 3:30 in the morning to support Elephant who was in the process of being overrun. When I arrived in the area, Candlestick was there flaring the battle scene. The scene was low overcast, probably up to around 2,000 to 3,000 feet solid, with a high overcast based at about 12,000 feet or so. We were unable to work visually in the area at all...."*

Because of weather conditions, all strikes made in support of Elephant had to be directed in by the Marine TPQ ground directed radar bombing system located at Khe Sanh. The FAC reported: [31]

> *"Candlestick and I were flying through the layers; Candlestick flaring at the request of Elephant. Elephant reported he was under heavy ground attack. He reported tanks and trucks coming down Route 9 from west to east. His outer perimeter had already been breached, and he was calling for air strikes.*

> "Since we were unable to define the situation on the ground, all we could do was to take coordinates given to us by Elephant and relay them to Alleycat (Night ABCCC) and have them TPQ it with Carstairs Bravo (Marine control at Khe Sanh). Even if the TPQs were pinpoint in accuracy, the problem here was that the NVA were moving so fast that by the time the TPQs hit, they were probably well away from the target area and continuing with the attack.
>
> "We had two Yellowbirds (B-57s) in the area with fire bombs, but we could not expend them because we could not identify the battle on the ground. We just had to sit up there, rather frustrated, and TPQ to help them out. Just before dawn, Elephant reported that they were being overrun. I could hear the machine guns and mortars in the background as he talked rather sadly over the radio....."

Lt Col Soulang advised the FAC that he was going to have to evacuate the command post and retreat to the east toward the Lang Vei Special Forces Camp -- just across the border in South Vietnam.[32/] The BV-33 Commander later reported that he radioed for help to Lang Vei and requested helicopter airlift, but helicopters were not available. He then directed his people to evacuate on foot across the border toward Lang Vei. This group included 276 BV-33 troops, approximately 200 Meo troops, and approximately 2,300 refugees, some of whom were BV-33 dependents.[33/]

Midway, the BV-33 Commander contacted an indigenous soldier at Lang Vei and again asked for helicopter support. He was given an affirmative answer, but none arrived by 1700 hours. The refugees continued to move along Route 9.[34/] Their withdrawal was covered by air. The weather cleared slightly during the day, and while one FAC directed strikes in against the former Elephant command post, another FAC followed the refugees. Covey 263 located the refugees on the road, and began directing strikes in on bridges behind them.[35/] Probably due to these strikes, enemy pursuit was not aggressive.[36/]

Hillsboro ABCCC reported on the BV-33 withdrawal:[37/]

> *"Elephant had been overrun before Hillsboro (daylight call sign) took station and the survivors and refugees were travelling along Route 9 toward Khe Sanh. Covey FACs remained over the column throughout the day and saw them into the compound at Lang Vei. The presence of the FAC aircraft apparently prevented further harassment. Elephant reported three medium tanks supporting the battalion attacking him. FAC recced the area and reported tracks of some type of vehicle with cleated treads but found no tanks. Route 9 was interdicted and a bridge bombed for a precautionary measure after the refugees had proceeded west of it."*

An Army debriefing officer reported later on the BV-33 arrival at Lang Vei:[38/]

> *"Advanced platoon arrived at Lang Vei SF Camp, where they were disarmed as were rest of unit arriving later. Lt Col Soulang remonstrated with Commander of USSF, a Lt Col, who ordered that weapons be given back to BV-33. He then told BV-33 CO to deploy his unit in defense positions at Old Lang Vei Camp (approx 1,000 meters north of SF Camp). Refugees were herded to location approximately 800 meters east just off Rte 9. BV-33 stayed at their positions at Lang Vei and made several patrols accompanied by USSF personnel. BV-33 lost 1 officer, MIA, and two USSF on these patrols. After the 27th of January, adequate amounts of food were prepared, both rice and C-rations, but no arms, ammo, clothing nor shovels to dig adequate defense positions. Medical aid provided BV-33 WIA....."*

The Laotian soldiers and refugees were now in a zone of comparative safety, but only temporarily. Within two weeks, the Lang Vei Special Forces Camp would also be overrun and would no longer represent a haven. The attack on Elephant was the first indication of enemy armored vehicles being in the area. Although the BV-33 Commander was usually a reliable source of intelligence, his report of tanks was viewed with skepticism by some officials, primarily because there was no visual sighting of tanks prior to the Lang Vei attack. Tracks had been sighted, but these could have been made by vehicles other than tanks. Bad weather and camouflage techniques successfully masked the enemy's true intent. 39/

Loss of the Elephant camp meant the loss of a valuable intelligence source. Lt Col Soulang had often been able to advise the Covey FACs of enemy movement in the Route 9 area, and his forces had been the first to detect the enemy's construction of a new road bypassing Route 9 into Quang Tri Province. This new road, which was well concealed beneath the jungle canopy, was being constructed in the Co Roc Mountain area just south of Route 9. Some of the more lucrative targets struck in the Niagara effort were in the Co Roc Mountain area. 40/ During the period 7-17 January, BV-33 guerrilla teams operating southeast of Ban Houei Sane also discovered extensive enemy positions in vicinity of Co Roc Mountain (XD 741 316). Their observation was reported as follows: 41/

- On 11 January, a team found an occupied 50-man foxhole complex at the top of Co Roc Peak.

- On 13 January, a patrol observed 75 NVA soldiers and sighted heavy ground fire, including 50-caliber machine guns, firing at an aircraft.

On 15 January, a team observed a hut with a long wire antenna set up next to it. The area showed signs of heavy foot traffic in the immediate vicinity.

On 16 January, two caves were discovered, one of which contained two tons of rice. Three enclosed structures were located nearby which could house 30 men each. Approximately 900 meters SE of the caves, an extensive bunker complex was discovered. The team counted five hundred bunkers, and reported that many were of 10-man capacity. One large bunker was estimated to be for a regimental command post. The other bunkers were constructed with gun ports for defensive action.

Loss of the Elephant Camp reemphasized a lesson learned in the Vietnam conflict. When small friendly garrisons and outposts have been subjected to determined, heavy enemy assaults, tactical airpower has been essential to successful defense and/or evacuation. Under conditions favorable to the enemy, e.g. inclement weather, tactical airpower has not always been able to preclude them from being overrun. Radar directed strikes have helped to offset weather disadvantages in Vietnam, but such strikes are limited when forces are closely engaged. The impact of new weapons, such as wide area anti-personnel mines (WAAPM), on similar situations has yet to be determined. Similar attacks have been broken when defending forces were able to withstand the assault until the weather cleared, or when the defending forces called in strikes on their own positions. Of course, a larger fixed position such as Khe Sanh would be a different matter. Launching a major assault against positions such as Khe Sanh would mean the massing of enemy forces, thus making them extremely vulnerable to airpower -- especially when it was applied on a SLAM-type basis.

Although superior enemy forces usually had little difficulty overpowering small fixed positions in bad weather, their usual tactic was withdrawal rather than attempting to hold the position once it was abandoned by the occupants. This precluded effective air bombardment of the abandoned position, and quite often forced aircraft to expend on uncertain withdrawal route targets. However, enemy withdrawal and tactical air effectiveness in this particular situation presented a departure from the norm. Enemy objectives in the area offered limited withdrawal alternatives. Movement in any direction still placed the enemy in the NIAGARA targeting area, and the extensive application of B-52s and tactical airpower under the NIAGARA concept reduced the probability of escape.

NIAGARA and the Tet Offensive

Obviously, the attack on BV-33 was designed to eliminate surveillance of enemy movement in the area. Continued surveillance by the Covey FACs, the Special Forces at Lang Vei, and other outposts and patrols helped offset the loss of the BV-33 camp. Reports on heavy enemy movement in the area continued to be made. On the day the Elephant camp was evacuated, a Marine outpost three kilometers northwest of Khe Sanh reported that two rows of its defensive wire had been cut and replaced as to indicate it was undisturbed. On the same date, other outposts and patrols in the vicinity of the Khe Sanh combat base reported extensive enemy troop movement to the east on Route 9. Heavy enemy troop movement was also reported in the vicinity of Lang Vei. 42/

Refugee movement on Route 9 presented a problem. Covey FACs reported over 1,000 refugees on Route 9 from the Laotian border to Lang Vei, and in certain instances their presence helped protect enemy forces from air strikes. In one instance, a target 500 meters northeast of Lang Vei was passed to Hillsboro for immediate air strike. The target was described as a troop concentration and command post three miles southwest of Khe Sanh. A FAC in the area reported 200-300 refugees on Route 9, 500 meters from the target, and 500 more on a trail from the target to Route 9. The target was not struck because of the proximity of the refugees, and the possibility that the troop concentration was in actuality a group of refugees. Again, monsoon weather was favorable to enemy movement, and hindered visual confirmation. 43/

On 26 January, Covey 252 and another FAC were flying over the Special Forces Camp at Lang Vei, when the Elephant Commander and members of the Special Forces Group reported trucks moving down Route 9 toward their positions. As Covey 252 reported: 44/

> *"Of course, we foresaw a reenactment of the disaster at Elephant. We requested some napalm and CBU and a flareship, none of which were available. We ended up hitting the coordinates where the trucks were supposed to be located with some M-117s -- a flight of F-100s. We notified 7AF that we considered it necessary to have napalm and CBU available, to use on troop concentrations and vehicles."*

21

Khe Sanh was already effectively pinned down, with airlift being the only means of resupply and evacuation of personnel. The Marine base camp was under constant fire from enemy mortars, rockets, and artillery, and much of their own artillery ammunition had been destroyed when enemy rounds hit their ammo dump on 22 January. New enemy positions were springing up all around Khe Sanh defensive positions, with reinforcements continually moving into the area. It appeared that a major assault on Khe Sanh was imminent. In addition to other intelligence sources, an NVN officer who rallied at Khe Sanh airfield on 20 January said that "beginning with Khe Sanh, every U.S. base between the Laotian border and Con Thien is to be taken before Tet."[45/]

In view of the increased activity in I Corps, COMUSMACV contacted the American Ambassador and requested that the planned truce during the Tet Holidays be cancelled. Concomitantly, the 7AF Commander advised that enemy actions in the NIAGARA area were considered to be "preparatory to the main battle". He advised his Deputy Chief of Staff for Operations on 24 January:[46/]

> *"When the main thrust comes we will know it by the level of coordinated preparatory fire followed by assaulting enemy infantry. All the air we have available will be shuttled night and day. Our tactics will be predicated on that basis. Whenever it is possible, we should mass the B-52s and then follow with the TAC air. This has always been sound and we shouldn't get away from it here. This is the tactic I will propose to General Westmoreland when the main battle begins.*

> "The strikes Monday afternoon (22 January) against the 300 troops according to the refugees from Khe Sanh was far more effective than first report. According to reports given by these people at least four hundred or more NVA troops were killed by the CBU attack. We should continue to employ a balanced load of hard bombs and CBUs. The bombs to open up the canopy with CBUs to get exposed personnel. We will find in this battle more concentration of troops than has been the case in the past. Consequently, CBU-2s and 24s should be our primary weapon if the situation develops as described.

> "Again I want to be sure you fully understand my guidance on the total use of the forces. We must provide close air support to troops who are in contact. It doesn't matter where this is. These requirements will be met above all others. I construe troops in contact to also include helicopters, AC-47s or any other air vehicle which is engaging enemy troops. Since the battle in Khe Sanh may go for an extended time we must be in a posture to sustain our effort. Hold back our surge until I decide to make the all out effort.

> "We must continue with the interdiction in Laos and Rt Pkg I. Strikes in the North will be reduced when the weather is bad to bolster the interdiction effort in Laos. If the weather breaks we will go for a maximum effort in Laos providing there is not a crisis at Khe Sanh. If there is a crisis at Khe Sanh, it will take priority over all strikes in the North."

Further guidance was provided by the 7AF Commander on the 24th: [47/]

> "Until the enemy commits himself at Khe Sanh the level of effort should be balanced against the interdiction program in Laos. Particular attention should be given to Route 9. I expect this to be the main supply route. As soon as the refugees are cleared, and under FAC control to be sure of their clearance, I want to keep this route interdicted night and day. You should be working on it west of Elephant area now. Combat Skyspot should be utilized when the weather is bad.

> "First thing tomorrow morning (25 Jan) put strikes against the Elephant Airfield. This field should be kept knocked

> *out. I would also like to keep all potential operating locations for MIGs which are within range of the Khe Sanh area knocked out. We know the airfields, so it is a matter of coordination between ourselves and the Navy."*

From this point on, concentrated airpower would provide the primary defense for the Khe Sanh area. Weather was extremely unfavorable, but ground directed radar strikes would help offset this disadvantage. There was no shortage of lucrative targets, and the SLAM effort insured around-the-clock availability of strike aircraft. From 22 through 29 January, over 3,000 tactical strike sorties were flown into the NIAGARA area. Bomb damage assessment (BDA) for these strikes was reported as follows: 346 secondary explosions and fires, sixteen trucks destroyed and seven damaged, 18 gun positions destroyed and three damaged, 29 bunkers destroyed and ten damaged, 181 structures destroyed and 65 damaged, and 241 KBA. This BDA was reported by visual sighting, and is undoubtedly deflated in view of the extremely bad weather at the time. Well over 200 B-52 sorties were also flown in NIAGARA during this period.[48/] Even approximate BDA on these strikes was prohibited by severe weather conditions and the lack of ground follow-up. ARC LIGHT BDA will be discussed later in this study.

On the day before Tet, the Vietnamese Government cancelled the 36 hour ceasefire throughout South Vietnam.[49/] In the NIAGARA area on the 29th, reports from special air delivered sensors indicated "a lot of activity in Khe Sanh area". These reports said further:[50/]

> *"Many troop movements of large and small units from Laotian border as far south as ten miles below Khe Sanh. All movements toward Khe Sanh. Seems to be big push."*

Then, the enemy launched his widespread Tet Offensive. While maintaining pressure against friendly positions in the NIAGARA area, the enemy struck Saigon, Hue and 34 of 45 provincial capitals, and numerous U.S. and Vietnamese military installations.[51/] Demands upon airpower during the Tet Offensive emphasized more than ever the need for centralized control of all air resources under the Deputy COMUSMACV for Air Operations. The foremost consideration facing the 7AF Commander was to insure airpower responsiveness to requirements generated by multiple widespread tactical situations, while maintaining the required weight of effort in Operation NIAGARA. On 30 January, the Commander directed that all air units maintain a 1.2 sortie rate and be prepared to surge upon his direction. He directed the following priority for the air effort:[52/]

- Adjust to meet live targets as first priority.

- Carrier forces to be directed against the enemy headquarters in NIAGARA and in support of Khe Sanh.

- Thailand-based forces to be applied against Laos LOCs (1) and in support of Khe Sanh (2).

- SVN-based 7AF resources to provide emergency support Pleiku and other Corps areas (1) and Khe Sanh (2).

- Marine forces: (1) Khe Sanh, (2) Camp Carroll, and (3) Emergency support.

Authority to frag and divert Thai-based strike aircraft into specific areas of South Vietnam, along with the planned input of carrier forces, helped provide adequate resources and the operational flexibility required to insure that the NIAGARA air effort was not diluted. The NIAGARA sortie rate during the initial Tet thrust shows clearly that Khe Sanh and Camp Carroll were not left exposed while airpower responded to other tactical requirements. For the first three days of the Tet Offensive, the sortie rate in the NIAGARA area was actually higher than it had been on the previous three days. 1,113 tactical strike sorties and 86 B-52 sorties were flown in NIAGARA during the three days prior to Tet, while 1,164 tactical and 123 B-52 sorties were flown the first three days of the offensive. 53/

Responsiveness was a requirement that impacted as much on FAC, reconnaissance and intelligence as it did on strike operations. Twice during NIAGARA, major shifts of emphasis were made to deal with critical tactical requirements. The first on 2 February entailed a 40-hour "crash" targeting effort designed to preempt enemy action against Camp Carroll, near the eastern edge of the NIAGARA area. The second, occasioned by the rocket bombardment of Tan Son Nhut that began on 18 February, required redeployment of FACs and an urgent redirection of the reconnaissance and targeting effort until the threat could be brought under control. Both these tasks were successfully accomplished without seriously impairing the targeting of the enemy threat to Khe Sanh, although they severely tasked the human and material resources available. 54/

By 2 February, the expected enemy assault against Khe Sanh had not developed. COMUSMACV estimated on 2 February that the attack would develop "tonight or tomorrow morning". He also anticipated an attempt by the enemy to overrun Camp Carroll at the same time. Accordingly, the 7AF Commander provided directions for the air effort:[55/]

> *"Weather will be bad in both areas. We need to increase our Sky Spot effort in both areas tonight and tomorrow. General Westmoreland also requested that we bring the Sky Spot in as close as we can. Coordinate this effort with the Marines to maximize the effort of the CSS.*
>
> *"CBUs are released for use in the same area. The restrictions set forth in MACV wire apply. Be prepared to use these weapons as requested or required. Alert three wings of possible use.*
>
> *"If attack at Khe Sanh/Camp Carroll does come tonight or tomorrow, I want to apply maximum effort as soon as the weather permits. Due to the other battles, we should plan on using as much effort from out of country forces as feasible. We should stay with the 100 sorties from the Navy with plans for requesting another 100 sorties. We should not lose sight of the possibility the enemy may launch other concerted attacks at Pleiku, Kontum, Quang Tri City, Hue, and conceivably, DaNang. Thus, there may be large demands at one time. In that case, we will use all out of country forces in SVN and thin out other requirements in the south."*

Concerning this possible major effort by the enemy, the following 7AF actions were taken to make optimum use of in-country forces:[56/]

- The force was notified to be prepared to go to an increased state of alert and surge as required.

- All CSS sorties were diverted, range permitting, to NIAGARA.

- For all TOTs (Time over Target) prior to 1200, 3 Feb, bases in range of NIAGARA (Phu Cat, Tuy Hoa, Cam Ranh, Phan Rang) would load hard ordnance for CSS. They

> would be launched on preplanned TOTs for better
> flow control. If Hillsboro could not handle the
> flight, it would proceed to fragged target. Loads
> for afternoon would depend on weather outlook.

Again, the estimated enemy assault did not develop, and after the initial Tet thrust, priorities established by MACV did reduce the air effort in NIAGARA. This reduction was primarily to meet the support required in other Corps areas, and it applied to the support required from 7AF, Navy, and Marines, as well as the diversion of selected Arc Light sorties.[57/] From 23 January through 1 February, there was a daily average of 429 tactical strike sorties flown in NIAGARA. For the next ten day period, the daily average was 219 sorties. Although there was some diversion of selected B-52 sorties, the daily rate actually continued at a higher level -- an average of 36 sorties per day from 23 January through 1 February, and a daily average of 38 for the next ten days.[58/]

The tactical sortie rate going into NIAGARA continued at a substantial level. Although a major push against Khe Sanh did not develop during the initial Tet thrust, the enemy forces still represented a threat. Khe Sanh was completely surrounded and under constant artillery, rocket and mortar bombardment. This fire was coming from virtually all directions, including the village of Khe Sanh, which the enemy had occupied at will. Monsoon weather was still in the enemy's favor, and it was known that he had the capability to launch a mass assault; however, to do so would make his forces more vulnerable to airpower. Thus, the tempo of air operations was maintained at a high level.[59/]

The Fall of Lang Vei

Although there was more than sufficient advance notice that the Special Forces Camp at Lang Vei would come under heavy attack, probably backed by armored support, the enemy appeared to have little difficulty in overrunning this outpost on 7 February. An Assistant Platoon Leader in the 304th NVA Division rallied to the Lang Vei camp on 30 January, and stated that Lang Vei was to be overrun. The interrogation report said: [60/]

> *"Source stated his battalion, the 8th, began infiltrating in September 1967. During infiltration, the battalion was hit by B-52 strikes and lost 50 per cent of its strength to casualties, many more to desertion, and returned to NVN for replacements. His unit, subordinate to the 66th Regt, arrived in the Khe Sanh area on 20 January and on 21 January attacked the district headquarters there. Again, the battalion lost over half its strength and now has a strength of about 200 men. They are deployed immediately west of Khe Sanh village near Route 9 (XD 839383) awaiting orders to overrun the Lang Vei camp. The battalion command post and an unidentified part of the 66th Regt are in artillery-proof bunkers. Although source heard of no outside support, he stated that the 304th NVA Division is to 'help take the Khe Sanh Combat Base'."*

This source, of course, could have represented an enemy strategem, but there were even more reliable indications that Lang Vei would be attacked. Special "Igloo White" sensors detected considerable personnel and vehicle movement toward Lang Vei, and patrols and outposts continued to report heavy enemy activity in the area. Both Elephant and the Special Forces Commander had reported the same information.

The radio call sign for the Lang Vei Special Forces Camp was "Spunky Hanson", a name equally familiar to Air Force Covey FACs as that of "Elephant". Coveys flying in the NIAGARA area were in daily radio contact with the Special Forces Camp, and these pilots felt a strong personal involvement on the morning of 7 February when the urgent call came over the radio that "Spunky Hanson" was under heavy ground assault. 61/

First indications of the attack came on the previous evening. At approximately 1840 hours on 6 February, "Spunky Hanson" reported receiving heavy high-angle enemy fire. Four hours later, the Marine Base at Khe Sanh came under heavy artillery, rocket and mortar bombardment; simultaneously, the Marine outpost on Hill 861 overlooking Khe Sanh reported an enemy ground probe. Then, shortly after midnight, the urgent call came from "Spunky Hanson" that Lang Vei was under attack from a large enemy force supported by tanks and flamethrowers. 62/

A flareship and Covey 235 were on station directing tactical air strikes against the enemy forces; however, the strike aircraft in the area at the time were loaded with hard ordnance, which was not too effective in this particular situation. Covey 235 had expended his flares and rockets, and a relief had been scrambled from Da Nang Air Base at approximately 0015 hours. The relief, Covey 232, who had Covey 280 in the right seat of his O-2 aircraft, arrived on the scene approximately 45 minutes later. Covey 232 described the situation: 63/

> "...Weather was not the best. The southern half of Lang Vei was anywhere from 1200 to 1000 feet broken, but mostly overcast. The northern half was about the same, mostly 1200 broken. We had a flareship on station, 'Basketball', who was doing as good as he could under the weather conditions. The ground fire was very heavy, extensive, making it almost impossible to stay in one position, because the minute you did they had you under fire. Artillery was also firing into the area from Khe Sanh. I received one set of fighters, Yellowbird 59 (B-57s), right after I made the request...."

When Covey 232 arrived on the scene, "Spunky Hanson" was on the radio. Covey 232 identified himself, and "Spunky Hanson" reported excitedly: 64/

> "We have tanks in the area! We have tanks in the area! I have one tank on top of my TOC at this time, there's another tank trying to enter the gate, coming into the compound, and I think there is another one coming down the road. Forget the one on top of the TOC, but see if you can hit the one coming through the gate, and the one coming down the road!"

That was the last contact Covey 232 had with "Spunky Hanson". "They were trapped in their bunker, and apparently their equipment was damaged, and they had to go off the radio," the FAC recalled. This loss of communications made a bad situation worse. The camp was practically overrun at this time, and without communications with the ground, it was impossible to adequately differentiate between friendly and enemy ground forces. 65/

Using a POL fire as navigational reference, the FAC located the tanks that "Spunky Hanson" requested struck. After Covey marked the targets with rockets, Yellow Bird 59 expended his ordnance destroying both tanks and obtaining 15 secondary explosions. Covey was hindered from directing strikes into the compound itself because he had lost contact with "Spunky Hanson" and could not determine the exact ground situation. He was then given instructions by the ABCCC to move out of the area to enable the Marines to fire artillery against the attacking force at Lang Vei. Covey 232 moved back from the area and assisted by spotting for the artillery. 66/

ABCCC "Moonbeam", an additional control aircraft staged from Udorn especially for NIAGARA night operations, reported: "When Carstairs II advised all air in the Lang Vei area to withdraw while 'Firecracker' (special Marine ordnance) was executed, air was withdrawn as directed but strikes continued in all other locations in support of the rest of the Khe Sanh area. Upon completion of 'Firecracker', no agencies were able to establish radio contact with Lang Vei; since friendlies were known to be in Lang Vei it was not possible to conduct additional visual or CSS strikes in extremely close air support roles of the camp." 67/

Later, as dawn approached, Covey 688 from Ubon was on the scene supporting relief operations. The enemy had completely overrun the camp by this time, and the Special Forces defenders were trapped in their command post bunker. An element of the BV-33 battalion advised by a U.S. Army Special Forces NCO were moving in from the old Lang Vei site in a rescue attempt. Covey 252, who joined Covey 688 at 0800 hours, defined the situation at this point: 68/

> "Our advisors (Spunky Hanson) were trapped in the TOC bunker in the middle of the camp, and the NVA were swarming all over it, throwing satchel charges and smoke bombs down through the vent. The relief forces, 'Spunky Hanson 15-Alpha,' which I understand were led by Special Forces Sergeant Ashley had moved up from the old Lang Vei Camp. But they were now pinned down by NVA machine gun fire.
>
> "Covey 688 was in contact with 15-Alpha. He had a Canasta flight, Navy A-1s, on station. There was an overcast at the time, about 500 feet base, up to about 1500-2000 foot, with very few holes in it. Also a high overcast up to about 4,000 feet. 15-Alpha, who was in contact with the trapped forces, requested that the A-1s attempt strafing passes against the enemy surrounding the bunker. The A-1s also had 250 lb and 500 lb bombs, and some napalm."

With the Canasta A-1s in trail, Covey 688 led them through the clouds to the target, describing it as best he could. With the FAC "talking" them into the target, the A-1s were able to effectively strafe the TOC. They then remained below the 500 foot overcast in hilly terrain and continued to make strafing passes in support of the trapped forces. Covey 252, who was still on station monitoring the situation, reported: 69/

> "...15-Alpha several times mentioned he was having trouble getting the BV-33 people with him to advance against the enemy forces and the TOC. He mentioned at one point that he practically had to use gun point to get them to move. 15-Alpha went back to the old camp alone and returned with a 57-mm recoilless rifle. He was able to silence a couple of machine gun nests with it...."

At this point, the weather began to break, allowing the A-1s to effectively expend their bombs and napalm. They began conducting strikes on the west side of the camp. Although these strikes resulted in several fires and explosions, the NVA forces still managed to keep several of their machine gun positions in operation. 70/

Covey 252 took over from 688 after the Canasta flight completed its strikes and returned to base. Two Air Force A-1s, Hobo 01 and Hobo 02, arrived on station with CBU, napalm, and 20-mm, and Covey 252 began directing them on strikes in the western perimeter. The objective was to suppress fire at the western end of the camp, while 15-Alpha attempted to storm the TOC. Covey reported that the Hobos were right on target, and "were flying through their own napalm smoke" to suppress the enemy fire. Although this suppressive fire was provided, the trapped men still were not rescued at this time because the BV-33 forces still reportedly refused to storm the TOC. 71/

Shortly afterwards, a 50-man heliborne relief force led by Army Special Forces personnel from the Khe Sanh Combat Base was dispatched with the mission of joining with the BV-33 unit in a raid on the camp. Gunships and tactical air continued to conduct strikes on the TOC and surrounding area at Lang Vei in preparation for the raid. Under cover of this fire and prior to the arrival of the relief force, the friendly personnel on site took escape and evasion action. 72/

The relief force put down at old Lang Vei and moved overland to the new Lang Vei site. Enroute, they encountered 13 U.S. personnel who had been in the camp at the time of the initial attack. 73/ Advancing into the camp under protective artillery fire and air strikes, this force was able to recover the remaining personnel. 74/

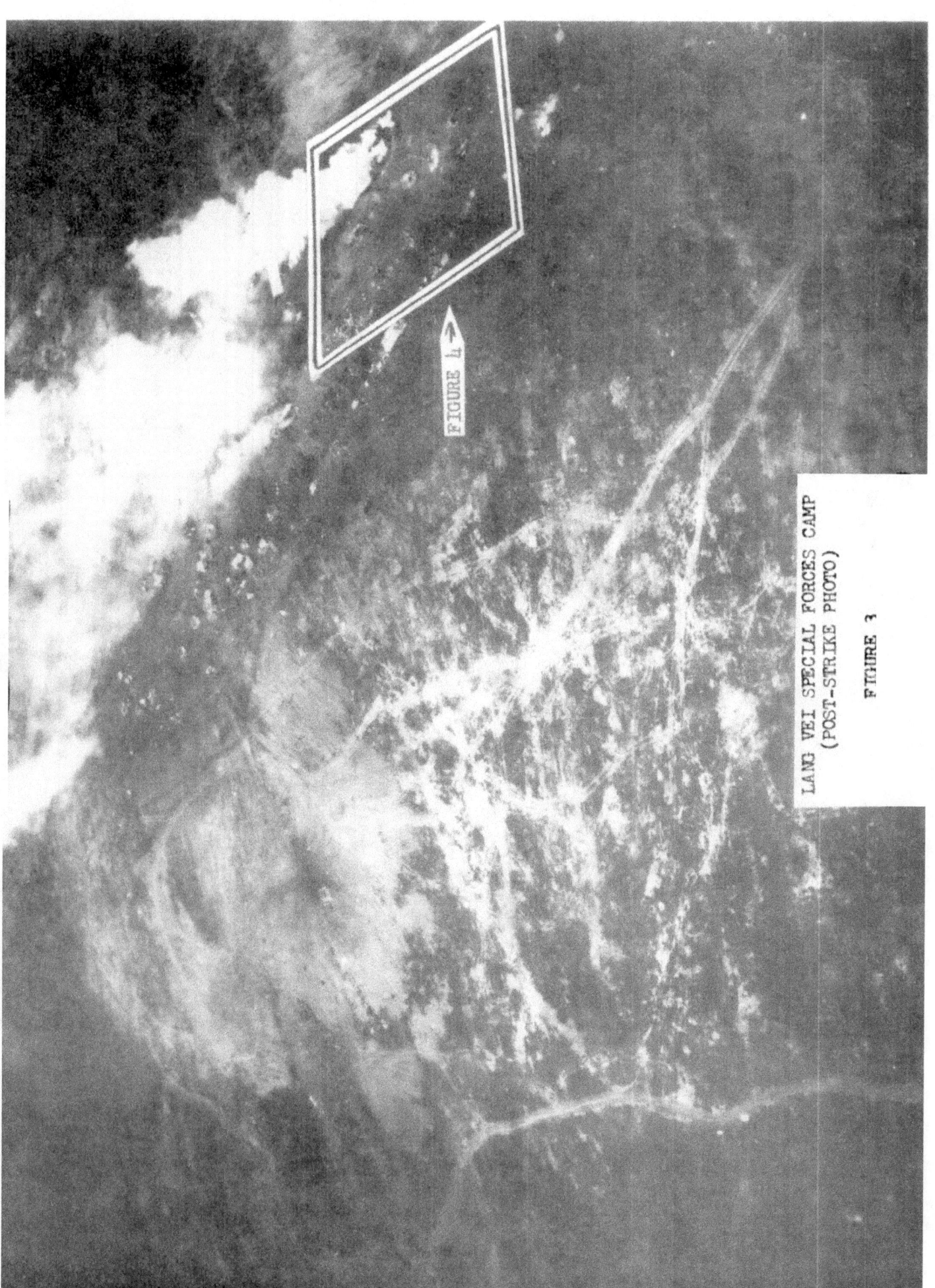

LANG VEI SPECIAL FORCES CAMP
(POST-STRIKE PHOTO)

FIGURE 3

LANG VEI SPECIAL FORCES CAMP
(POST-STRIKE PHOTO)

FIGURE 4

It was later reported that nine PT-76 light amphibious tanks of Soviet manufacture had been engaged in the assault, and that five of these were eventually disabled or destroyed by air strikes. Aerial photography confirmed the use of PT-76 tanks and use of the Xe Pone River as approach route to Lang Vei. It was also reported that the attack on the camp was composed of an estimated enemy company supported by armored vehicles, including an armored personnel carrier. The defensive wire around the camp was not an effective barrier to the armored thrust. Reports from the Special Forces indicated that Cal .50 AP ammunition had no apparent effect on the armored vehicles, and the M-72 (Lightweight anti-tank weapon) was marginally effective, due to malfunction of some of these weapons. 75/

Covey 232 reported two important lessons learned in the Lang Vei attack. These were: 76/

- Covey 235, the FAC on station when the attack began, had an insufficient rocket load to meet the requirements of an intense situation such as the Lang Vei attack. With only one pod of rockets (seven rockets) he had expended much of his rocket supply directing fighters against earlier targets. Thus, when the enemy struck Lang Vei, he found his target marking capability severely limited. This was later brought to the attention of the Covey Operations Officer, and the Coveys flying into the area were loaded with an additional rocket pod and two flares.

- A series of unfortunate circumstances placed limitations on air support during the Lang Vei attack. Inclement weather decreased flareship effectiveness as well as FAC and strike operations. Not only did the FAC on station at the beginning of the attack find himself short of rockets, but the strike aircraft immediately available were armed with hard ordnance--heavy bombs for NIAGARA interdiction targets. The close ground

situation precluded the effective expenditure of
such ordnance. When the relief FAC arrived on
station, the situation was critical. Air support
at this point could have been more effective if
applied against the enemy forces closer to the
friendly troops-- possibly right on top of the friendly
troops who were trapped in bunkers. However, the FAC
could not do this without direction from the friendly
forces themselves, and he found himself without
radio contact with the ground. He did have radio
contact with "Spunky Hanson 15A", who was attempting
to rescue the trapped personnel, but "Spunky Hanson 15A"
was unable to give complete information as to their
location and could not provide clearance for close-in
strikes. Covey 235 recommended that outposts and
Special Forces Camps adopt a visual means of communication
for use at night in the event radio contact is lost.
Perhaps a ground flare system using various colors
to keep the FAC advised of the ground situation and
requirements could be adopted. As it turned out, the
most significant role played by air and artillery at
Lang Vei was to force temporary enemy withdrawal
allowing evacuation of friendly forces.

Earlier at the Khe Sanh Base Camp, the Air Force ALO had questioned how the camp would mark its lines for visual identification if air support were required in defense of the camp. Khe Sanh officials advised that at night they would use strobe lights. The ALO commented that at night, strobe lights looked just like muzzle flashes from small arms, and this was not the "best means" to mark their lines. He suggested: [77/]

> *"I requested that they use some type of flare, or perhaps a 55 gallon drum with fuel oil sunken in the ground so small arms would not penetrate. They could light these around their perimeter, and it was possible that this would penetrate even a low layer of fog. This would allow them to direct air strikes even under fog conditions. It took over three weeks to get any action taken on this. No action was taken until one of the FACs wrote up the problems that he encountered at Lang Vei where they had no way of directing airpower because of no visual reference to the ground..."*

The aftermath of Lang Vei's fall resulted in an unfavorable tactical situation--one which had tragic overtones. Khe Sanh, which was already crowded with some 6,000 Marines, ARVN soldiers and supporting personnel from other services, suddenly represented the only haven to several thousand refugees--both Laotian and South Vietnamese of various ethnic origins. Earlier, on 22 January, 1,050 refugees from Khe Sanh Village had been airlifed to more secure areas; however, many were required to remain behind. III MAF reported on this: 78/

> *"Commanding General, I Corps, General Lam, made decision that 5,000 - 6,000 Breu who desired to be evacuated from Khe Sanh could not be permitted to do so. The official reason given was that there is no place to relocate them nor any available foodstuffs to feed them. Unofficially, however, it is felt that the age old animosity between the Montagnards and the Vietnamese was a motivating factor behind General Lam's decision. Approximately 10,000 pounds of rice available at Khe Sanh was distrivuted to the Breu there to alleviate their hunger."*

Another Marine report stated that during the period 25 January - 8 February 1968, some 3,000 - 4,000 Breu (Montagnard) tribesmen "congregated in the village near the Khe Sanh Combat Base". The reasons given for not evacuating them were: (1) the problem of identifying Viet Cong (VC) sympathizers among them, and (2) the lack of a suitable location and food for them in a Quang Tri Province location away from the Khe Sanh area. Further, they were unable to return to their hamlets which had come under NVA control. 79/

In the past, the enemy had not been above using local villagers as shields for their assualts. Although this situation did not develop at

Khe Sanh, the Covey FACs reported on the situation facing the Marine Commander at Khe Sanh: [80/]

> *"They have a lot of Breu tribesmen, Montagnards, at Khe Sanh. Troops, not the refugees. Many of these refugees outside the camp are dependents or friends of the troops inside. They either elected or had to stay outside the base perimeter, therefore on their own, and at the mercy of the NVA. A logical application by the NVA in this circumstance would be to take the Breu families and charge the camp with the refugees in front. Naturally, the Breu troops would not fire on them, and if we fired on them, the Breu tribesmen inside would probably fire on us...."*

The 3rd Marine Division reported the following developments concerning the refugees during February: [81/]

> *"The Breu problem was compounded by an influx of Lao refugees, Lao military personnel, Mike Force and CIDG personnel from the Laotian border area and/or from Lang Vei into the Khe Sanh area due to the deterioration of the combat situation along the border. Ninety-one Lao military and civilians were airlifted from Khe Sanh to Da Nang on 29 January while 90 Mike Forces and CIDG personnel were evacuated by the same means on 28-29 January. The remainder of the Lao refugees returned to their country when the tactical situation permitted.*
>
> *"On 10 February the Breu tribal leader, Mr. Anya, four Breu village chiefs and their families (a total of 30 persons) were air-evacuated from Khe Sanh to Quang Tri via Da Nang. On 13 February, approximately 1,400 Breu walked from Khe Sanh to the Ca Lu area to escape heavy fighting in Huong Hoa District. Arrangements were made to guide them from Ca Lu to the Cam Lo Refugee Center, for resettlement, by a foot march via the Balong Valley and Route 558. On 17 February, 1,150 of the Breu refugees began their march and arrived at Cam Lo on 19 Febuary. They were joined by additional Breu traveling the same route during the period 20-23 February. At the end of that period, the number of Breu who had relocated from Khe Sanh to Cam Lo totaled 1,990.*

> "On 16-17 February some 2,000 to 4,000 Breu attempted to displace from Khe Sanh to Ca Lu to escape the fighting but were intercepted by the NVA at XD 882 399 and were turned back to their villages along Route 9 west of Khe Sanh. Some of these people were the relatives and families of the indigenous military personnel assisting in the defense of the Khe Sanh Combat Base. The presence of these Breu civilians in villages west of Khe Sanh constituted a serious detriment to 3d Marine Division artillery fires along the axis of Route 9. Arrangements were being made, as February ended to air evacuate those Breu who desired to do so from Khe Sanh as airlift became available."

For the second time in two weeks, the Laotian BV-33 soldiers and villagers felt the brunt of an enemy attack-- first, their own camp in Laos and now the Lang Vei Special Forces Camp. The following log of events as related by the BV-33 Commander to the U.S. Army Attache at Vientiane on 17 February best tells their side of the story: [82]

- **6 Feb 68**: Attack on Special Forces Camp began. On this day BV-33 issued approximately 24 hand grenades. The U.S. Camp overrun by enemy tanks and many U.S. Special Forces trapped in command bunker.

- **7 Feb 68**: One U.S. Special Forces personnel escaped to BV-33 and requested BV-33 help. Col Soulang sent a company to the U.S. Camp and was able to rescue approximately 7 U.S. Special Forces personnel including U.S. LTC who was seriously wounded. Enemy had not occupied camp but had pulled back approximately 300 meters to avoid artillery fire and air strikes. BV-33 then radioed Xom Cham (Khe Sanh) for evacuation helicopters. U.S. Special Forces Major at Xom Cham stated he would send two helicopters, one for U.S. and one for BV-33 but when helicopters arrived they picked up only U.S. Special Forces and South Vietnamese. They did not return. At this time enemy mortar and artillery fire intensified. LtCol Soulang gave orders to his unit commanders that they were to break up into small groups and attempt to reach Khe Sanh if possible. If not, to try to evade into Laos. Later, a light observation plane was sighted and Lt Col Soulang made radio contact requesting evacuation helicopters. Two were dispatched and took two loads of BV-33 personnel to Khe Sanh. Upon return to Lang Vei, one helicopter picked up a number of Lao soldiers, other returned empty. Enemy shelling and firing was intense and there was no one left to pick up. BV-33 had lost approximately 26 from enemy fire and U.S. air strikes. Refugees had already arrived at Khe Sanh on foot. They had moved as soon as attack on Lang Vei had begun. The 40 men who were picked up by helicopter and 74 who walked to Khe Sanh were disarmed and placed in craters or holes holding approximately 15 to 20 men and guarded by U.S. Marines. They felt as if they were being treated as POWs. Lt Col Soulang alone was allowed to keep his side arm. No food was issued to either BV-33 or refugees.

- <u>8 Feb 68</u>: After Soulang remonstrated with a U.S. Special Forces Major, weapons were returned to the BV-33 personnel but they were required to remain outside the wire. No food on this day either except that U.S. soldiers and marines shared with them.

- <u>9-10 Feb</u>: Enemy mortars, rockets, and artillery rounds continue to fall and refugees and BV-33 still had not received any food. U.S. and SVN officers allegedly said existing rice not for Lao. Refugees decided on the 10th of February to try and return to Laos. They feared that they would die at Khe Sanh and preferred to die in Laos rather than Vietnam. Refugees walked back to Laos on Route 9 on the 10th.

- <u>11 Feb</u>: Lt Col Soulang and 113 personnel evacuated to Da Nang by C-130.

- <u>12-14 Feb</u>: BV-33 personnel were disarmed again at Da Nang but were fed, bathed, clothed, comfortably housed and treated well in all respects. Lt Col Soulang and two officers went to Saigon to contact Lao Embassy at this time. Wounded were taken care of. An Air Force Civic Action Team was primarily responsible for their efforts on behalf of BV-33.

- <u>15 Feb 68</u>: BV-33 evacuated from Da Nang to Savannakhet, Laos by Royal Laotian Air Force C-47 aircraft.

After hearing Lt Col Soulang's report, one high ranking Laotian military official, General Boun Pone, CG Tactique Sud, reportedly said that after what happened to BV-33 that the Laotian Forces Armee Royale "must consider South Vietnamese as enemy because of their conduct". He pointed out, however, that he was not too concerned with "what happened in the past", but rather "more interested in getting back as many refugees and BV-33 personnel as possible". Many evading members of BV-33 did eventually make their way back to friendly lines and were able to make contact with American agents in Laos. [83/] Others were not so fortunate Many of the refugees were either killed by NVN forces or pressed into porterage service for the enemy. [84/]

The Covey FACs observed the refugees on several occasions moving at various points between Khe Sanh and the Laotian border. On 8 February, Covey 252 was over Khe Sanh at approximately 0745 hours. He was advised by the Khe Sanh control agency that "people were walking from east to west", from Khe Sanh City toward Lang Vei. There were several hundred of them in small groups along the road, and the Marines were "seriously considering" directing artillery fire against them. Fortunately, Covey 252 suggested that he first take a closer look at these people. He was able to identify them as refugees, and they were not fired upon. [85/]

Heavy refugee movement continued on Route 9 over the next few days, and on several occasions the Covey FACs were able to make confirmation of the noncombatant role of these persons--thereby precluding the inadvertent direction of friendly fire against them. Unfortunately, the continued safety of the refugees could not be assured. It soon became obvious that many of them had not reached safety, but had been pressed into service by the NVA forces. A definite change in the pattern of movement on Route 9 was detected. Rather than walking in one direction towards Laos, the refugees were observed moving back and forth on the road; NVA soldiers were intermingled with them. The presence of the NVA soldiers presented a dilemma. 86/

It was obvious to the Covey FACs that the enemy forces were now using the refugees for porterage, as well as cover for continued military infiltration. The FACs still considered these groups of persons to be noncombatants, which obviated their being considered as a military target. Conversely, the Marine control agency at Khe Sanh advised the Coveys that the presence of NVA soldiers among these people represented a real threat to the security of Khe Sanh, and if these circumstances were allowed, the Route 9 situation could grow considerably worse. Thus, the Marine control agency made the decision to direct fire into the area. Several secondary explosions on the road confirmed the presence of military stores. This regrettable situation was considered a personal tragedy by many of the FACs. Before the Elephant camp had fallen, the Coveys had often flown into the camp and had become friends with the camp commander and his people. The FACs' families in the United States had often sent gifts of clothing for distribution among the Laotian dependents. 87/

After the fall of Lang Vei, it appeared even more likely that an enemy assault against Khe Sanh was forthcoming. A COMUSMACV assessment on 10 February said: "Attacks by elements of up to six regiments are probable against Khe Sanh. These attacks can be supported by artillery, rockets, mortars, and a few armored vehicles. Interrogation of returnees indicates attacks throughout the DMZ will be supported by tanks and aircraft. The recent use of tanks at Lang Vei indicates the enemy may introduce new equipment and tactics to support offensive activity in I Corps." 88/

A 7AF Intelligence Report advised: "It appeared at first as if the attack on Lang Vei might be the first of a series of assaults along Route 9. Now the situation is unclear. The enemy has delayed considerably in following up his success at Lang Vei with an attack on Khe Sanh. There have been several vigorous attacks against the high ground to the north of Khe Sanh, particularly Hill 861. It is possible that the enemy is reluctant to undertake to overrun Khe Sanh without first securing the high ground around it." 89/

Attack Against Hill 861

Marine outposts around Khe Sanh were subjected to continuous harrassment from enemy mortar fire and ground probes. One of the more significant ground attacks was made on 8 February against an outpost on Hill 861 immediately north of Khe Sanh. Just prior to this attack, Covey 251 and Covey 252 had arrived in the area at approximately 0745 hours, had checked in with the ABCCC, and were reconnoitering refugee movements on Route 9. 90/

In response to a request from the Marine control agency at Khe Sanh, the FACs moved away from Route 9 to direct strikes against mortar and rocket positions on a ridgeline approximately one kilometer from the Khe Sanh runway. Canasta 403, a flight of four Navy A-1Hs, were on station with Mk-81s, Mk-82s, and 20-mm. The Coveys directed the Canasta flight on one bombing run against the ridge, received one secondary explosion, and then "held them high" when Khe Sanh radioed that they had lost contact with the outpost on Hill 861. [91/]

Covey 252 received the outpost coordinates from Khe Sanh, and immediately flew over the area. He first observed several men huddled in trenches. The FAC recalled: [92/]

> *"I couldn't really tell whether they were friendly or enemy troops, because the color of the uniforms all looked the same. They looked like our people, but there was always the possibility that our people had been overrun and were attempting to regain their positions. As remote as this was, it was still a possibility, and it prevented us from making immediate strikes."*

Khe Sanh control finally gave clearance for the FACs to direct strafing and bomb runs on the northwest base of the hill which was in defilade from Khe Sanh's suppressive fire. According to the FAC, the suppressive fire from Khe Sanh was effective except for the backside of the hill, where the enemy were actually located. The FAC described the Canasta 403 strikes: [93/]

> *"They did a fantastic job of placing their bombs and strafing passes right up the hill toward the outpost. While attacking, they would suppress the NVA fire, but as soon as I would hold them off, to survey our effectiveness,*

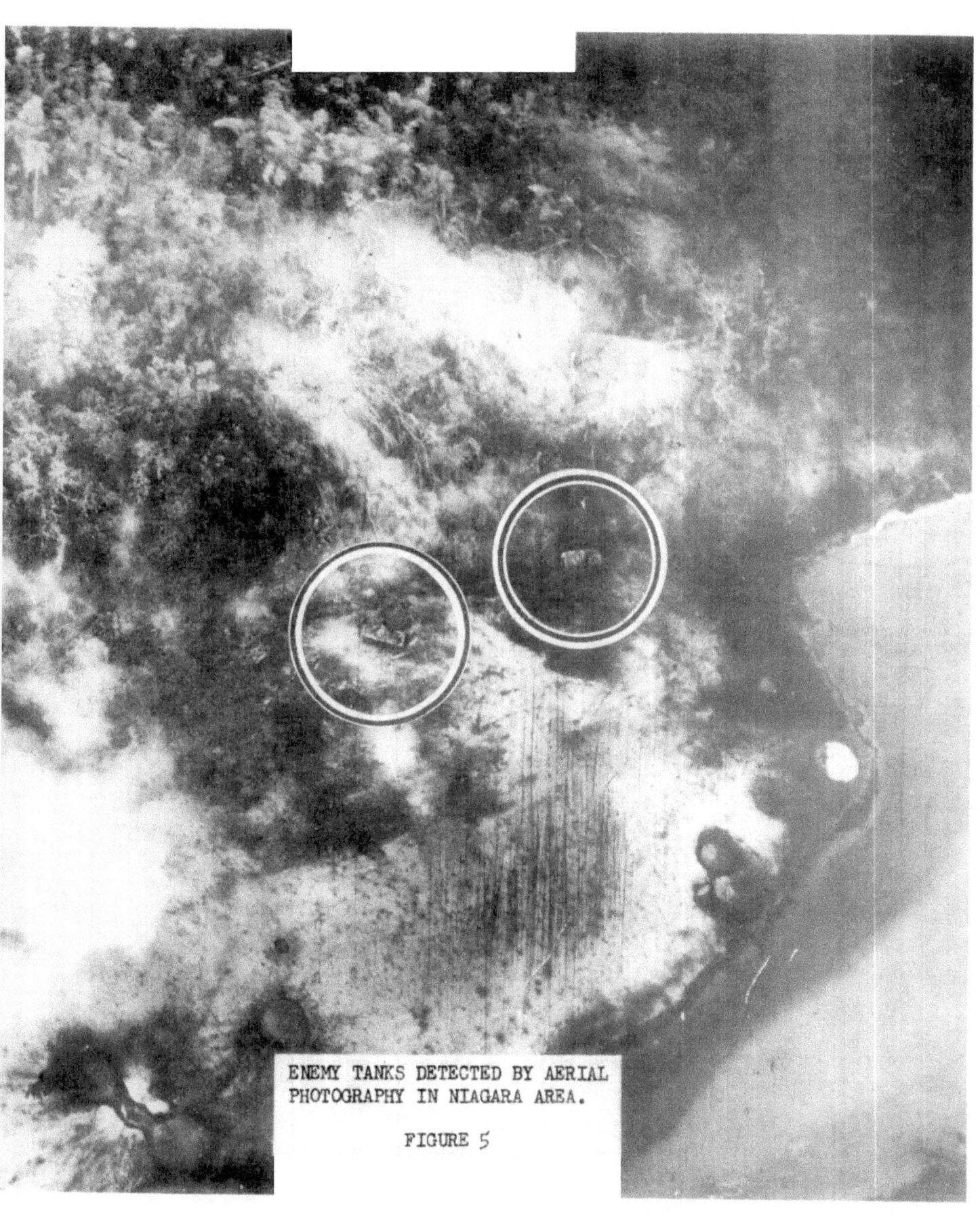

ENEMY TANKS DETECTED BY AERIAL PHOTOGRAPHY IN NIAGARA AREA.

FIGURE 5

> *the attack would resume. We then requested Spooky and some A-4s. We wanted napalm, CBU, and rockets.*
>
> *"We wanted any propeller driven aircraft available, to remain close to the target at low altitudes. In our opinion the outpost was in the process of being overrun, and if we didn't get air, it would be."*

As reported by Hillsboro, the weather was unworkable for jets, and the proximity of friendly troops prevented Sky Spot directed strikes. Task Force Alpha at Nakhon Phanon AB, Thailand immediately scrambled a flight of three A-26s, call signs Nimrod 32A, 34A, and 35A, to aid the outpost. Three T-28 "Zorros" from Nakhon Phanom were already airborne on armed reconnaissance in the STEEL TIGER area, and these were immediately diverted into NIAGARA by the ABCCC. Both the Zorros and the Nimrods arrived in time to repulse the attack. The Zorros were credited with 5 KBA confirmed, and the Nimrods with 45 KBA confirmed. [94/] The FAC reported on their effectiveness: [95/]

> *"Both flights were extremely effective. The A-26s just about saved the situation immediately with their area coverage, their strafing passes, their napalm, etc. When the Nimrods completed their passes, the attack was suppressed--enough so that the men in the outpost could stand up and walk off the hill without receiving fire. Apparently, they were in the process of evacuating the outpost at the time. APCs from Khe Sanh had arrived, and they were actually leaving the outpost. However, when the firing ceased, they decided to return to the hill. They went over the hill, captured several crew served weapons and small arms, and counted over 50 enemy KBA."*

Targeting and Tactical Response

When the 8 February attack against Hill 861 was repulsed, the enemy buildup in the Khe Sanh area had already reached its peak; however, no major ground engagement followed. Ground contact beyond the covering fires of the camp perimeter did continue, and attacks by fire against Khe Sanh became continuous.[96/] That enemy forces in the area still represented a major threat was made clear on 23 February when the Khe Sanh area reportedly received 1,000 rounds of artillery, mortar, and rocket fire in one five hour period.[97/] Concomitantly, the sustained air effort continued at a high level.[98/]

Equally as unprecedented as the sustained strike effort in the NIAGARA area was the intensive and carefully managed reconnaissance targeting cycle that made an effective round-the-clock air offensive possible.[99/] Within 40 hours after the 7AF Commander was tasked by COMUSMACV to initiate NIAGARA II SLAM operations on 31 January, a NIAGARA Intelligence Control Center was activated by the 7AF DCS/Intelligence and began generating sufficient tactical targets from an all source data base to assign specific objectives for the entire force. All out-country intelligence programs, except essential ones, were halted to maintain this special capability.[100/]

The primary objective of this task force was defined as follows:[101/]

> *"... to locate, identify, confirm and nominate for attack tactical targets in the NIAGARA area, assess the effects of attacks against these targets and determine reattack requirements."*

Many targets were visually acquired and struck. Reports of these strikes, added to other FAC sightings, provided a valuable input to the

NIAGARA Control Center. The Control Center in turn, provided a current and complete picture of known enemy dispositions around Khe Sanh. Effective application of the total air effort depended on the validity of that "picture." The defense of Khe Sanh became, to this extent, dependent on the generation of valid targets in Saigon, 375 miles away. Tan Son Nhut Air Base, with its photo processing and exploitation, and array of supporting intelligence capabilities, became the source of air targeting data for the entire effort. Later debriefing of the Officer in Charge (OIC) of the Regimental Fire Support Center revealed that NIAGARA Control's Hot Item Reports and nightly computer runs were employed in laying on artillery and Marine close-in air support as well. [102/]

A variety of resources were exploited to build the target data base. One primary source was the Human Intelligence (HUMINT) collection program-- interrogation of POWs and other local sources. Some of the earliest definitive information on enemy plans for Khe Sanh came from human source intelligence. From 22 January through 31 March, an Air Force interrogation team based at DaNang submitted approximately 100 special reports responsive to 7AF, MACV and PACAF requirements. One of the first examples covered the interrogation on 19 January of an NVA First Lieutenant. He provided the DaNang team with information on the enemy's offensive planning. He reported plans for a division-sized attack against Khe Sanh, the movement of tanks into the DMZ area for employment in SVN, and plans for attacks on other Marine DMZ positions. Reports of this kind were passed directly to NIAGARA ICC, where an all-source effort was operative to translate them into air targets. Reported bivouac areas, supply points and command posts, once plotted on maps, were researched in photography. Often, new reconnaissance was flown to exploit HUMINT data.[103]

A variety of specialized sensors, combining electronic, seismic and acoustic techniques, also provided inputs. The information was necessarily fragmentary--the precise location and nature of the types of activity detected required skilled interpretation or more often, educated guesswork. The unique value of the sensors was that they operated 24-hours a day throughout the enemy occupied area.[104]

Each intelligence source in its own way penetrated the tree and cloud cover which so often frustrated photo reconnaissance. The full value of the entire range of intelligence sources and special sensors was realized in NIAGARA under the impact of an intensive all-source intelligence effort. Separate inputs acquired increasing value as they were combined with other data, adding together to define new targets.[105]

Eventually, all target data was reduced to precise locations identified on photography. Target folders were then prepared for FACs and strike crews, and accurate eight-digit UTM coordinates provided for Arc Light and artillery use.[106]

The amount of aerial reconnaissance flown during Operation NIAGARA almost doubled the film footage normally processed by 7AF facilities. As the workload passed 100,000 feet of film per day, a 70 per cent augmentation

FIGURE 6

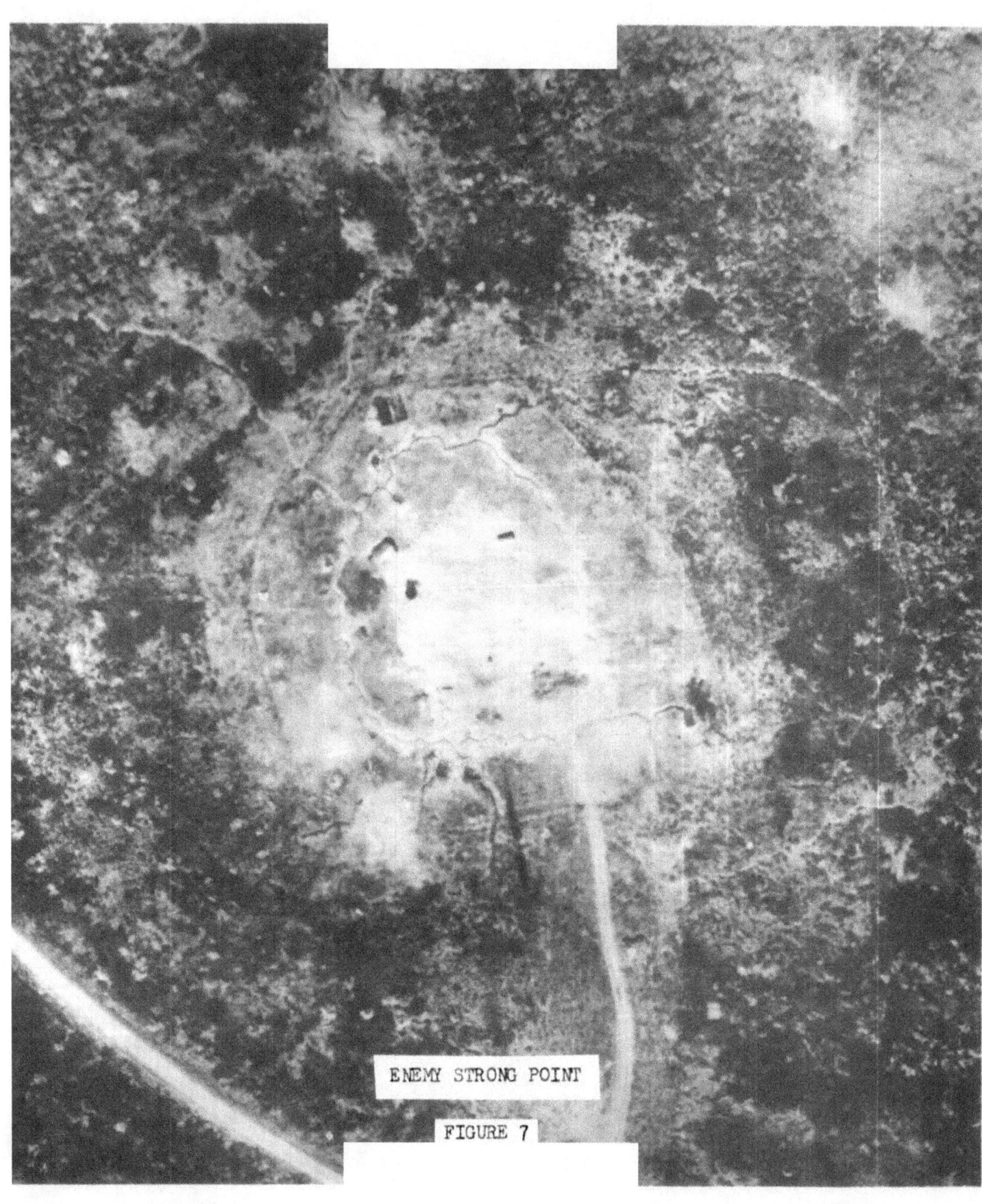

ENEMY STRONG POINT

FIGURE 7

FIGURE 8

in Photo Interpreter (PI) strength was effected. This permitted a 24-hour operation at full strength of 50 PI's and included both Air Force and TDY Army personnel.[107/]

Although the NIAGARA photo exploitation effort was large, there was evidence that it was still not large enough to capitalize on the available reconnaissance. During February, adverse weather cut total reconnaissance sorties in half. With twice as much time to exploit available imagery, the interpreters found nearly four times as many targets as in any other period. The "lesson learned" in this case was that the interpretation capability was seriously out-paced by the volume of reconnaissance flown.[108/]

A special report by Hq 7AF, DIPA, explained that the Intelligence Task Force provided centralized management of the entire intelligence effort for NIAGARA.[109/] This Task Force was responsible for determining intelligence requirements and priorities which facilitated the efforts of the Deputy for Operations and the Director, TACC, in their employment of the reconnaissance force supporting NIAGARA. The entire reconnaissance effort in NIAGARA was centrally controlled by the Director, TACC, with a single objective--to locate the enemy so the full impact of airpower could be brought to bear against him, in the defense of Khe Sanh. This produced the most intensive tactical reconnaissance program initiated to date in the war in SVN.

Requirements for tactical reconnaissance during Operation NIAGARA were so critical that missions were flown even if there was only a 5 - 8 percent chance of success. Despite inclement weather which prevailed throughout most of the operation, 90 percent of all sorties fragged were flown; 1,616 reconnaissance sorties were fragged and 1,453 were flown. These covered 1,994 reconnaissance objectives which ranged in size from pinpoint ground locations to large areas involving several hundred square miles.

The management of intelligence resources and the orderly flow of materials for this massive targeting effort required a task organization that was autonomous with respect to the regular intelligence staff and its routine workload. To provide this, the NIAGARA Intelligence Control Center at Tan Son Nhut had immediate access to imagery interpreters and their materials, and direct support from other 7AF intelligence agencies. At its peak, the NIAGARA ICC was staffed by 213 personnel drawn from various elements of Seventh Air Force, 7/13AF, MACV, the Philippines, Hawaii and CONUS. 110/

NIAGARA Control profited from the in-place 7AF Intelligence Data Handling System (IDS). Adapting existing resources, IDHS published the first Niagara Target List within 18 hours of its activation. Thereafter, a daily up-date target list was produced and transmitted to MACV, to the 26th Marine Regiment Fire Support Center at Khe Sanh, and to the 7AF strike planners. The file eventually covered over 2,000 targets, with entries detailing target identity, strike history, BDA and reconnaissance coverage.

The "Niagara File" then was integrated into the "in-country" target data base.[111]

As a result of this reconnaissance effort, 623 major targets were produced for strike aircraft--a rate of 1.4 targets per reconnaissance sortie. These findings collated with other intelligence resulted in 2,095 individual targets being nominated for strike. Nine hundred and seventy-eight were struck, 67 percent being attacked under CSS radar control. At the close of the operation, 1,483 targets had been deleted as a result of airstrikes and changes in status--from occupied to unoccupied--leaving 612 to be undertaken as part of the air support to be provided to the U.S. 1st Air Cavalry's counter-offensive operation in the area following the termination of NIAGARA on 31 March.[112]

A reconnaissance section was established in the Intelligence Control Center to manage each facet of the reconnaissance and imagery exploitation cycle of the targeting program. This office determined requirements and priorities and scheduled imagery exploitation. Optimum use was made of the full range of photographic sensors (black and white, color, camouflage detection, infrared and high acuity), as well as electronic systems. Sensor selection was based on operational factors and the capabilities of individual systems to meet specific reconnaissance requirements. Nearly a million feet of film was processed in the development of these targets.

Over half of the objectives were covered on black and white photography.[113/] Use of color and camouflage detection was governed by the nature of the targets and by the availability of supplies, processing equipment and the need for low level flights. Experience with regard to color and camouflage detection imagery in NIAGARA showed that for optimum utilization of these sensors:[114/]

- Color/Camouflage Detection should be flown between 1000-1500 hours.

- Area and route segment coverage should be restricted to locations of known or highly suspected activity.

- SAM, AAA, and AW sites are especially vulnerable to these sensors.

- They should be flown on relatively cloud free days and not over unbroken jungle canopy.

- In all instances, the lower the altitude the more productive the results.

By 27 January, the NIAGARA target development effort peaked at the rate of 300 targets in one day. The rate then leveled off. At its conclusion on 31 March, target development averaged 150 a day.[115/]

Many lucrative targets continued to be developed in the NIAGARA area although the estimated major assault against Khe Sanh did not materialize.[116/]

Among the unusual types of targets developed during NIAGARA were numerous caves, identified by intelligence as a possible enemy headquarters. The distinctive limestone formations of the Annamite Mountains lent themselves to such use. Figures 9, 10, and 11 depict several of the more

CAVES PHOTOGRAPHED IN NIAGARA AREA 24 FEB 68

FIGURE 9

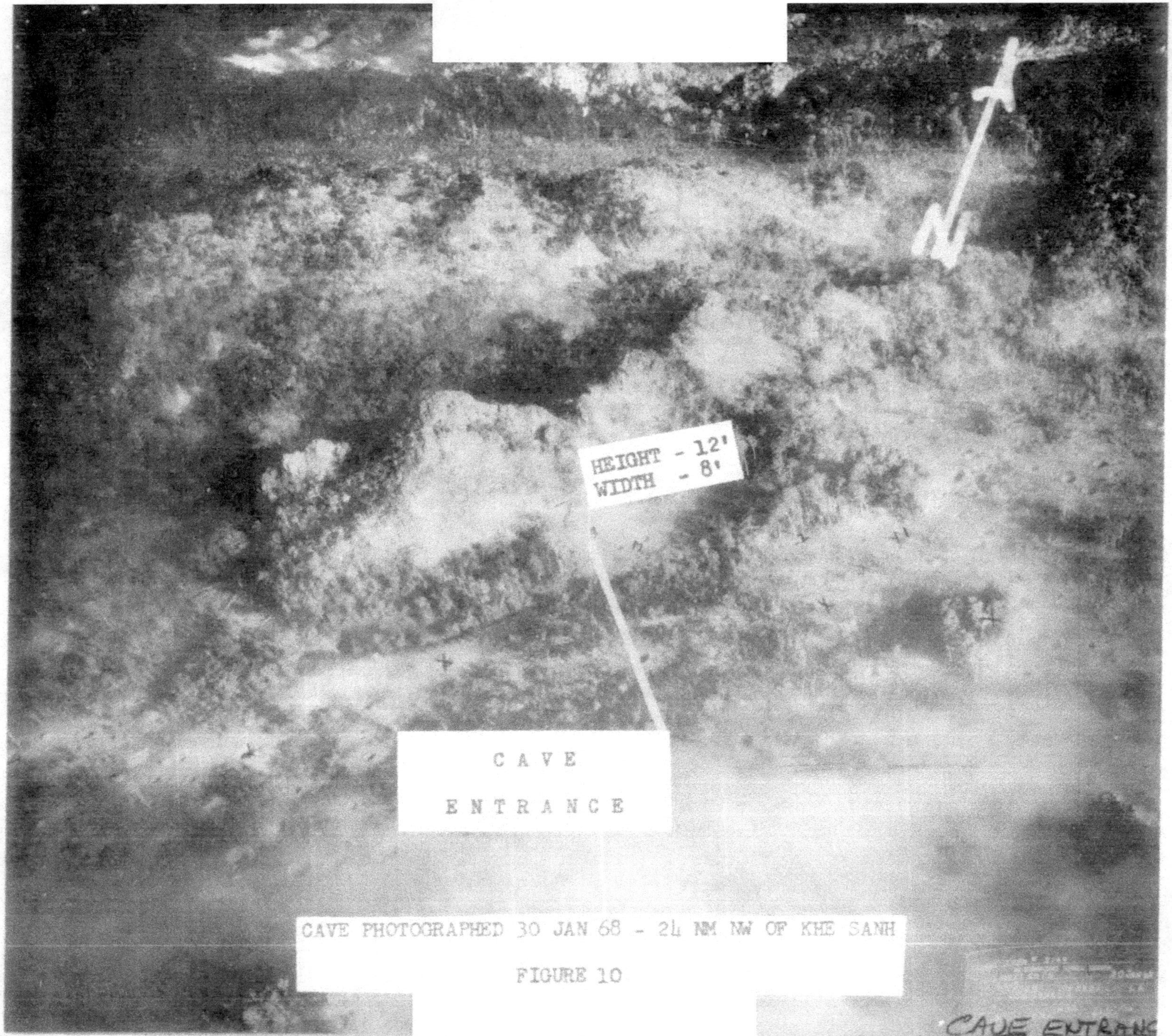

CAVE ENTRANCE

HEIGHT - 12'
WIDTH - 8'

CAVE
ENTRANCE

CAVE PHOTOGRAPHED 30 JAN 68 - 24 NM NW OF KHE SANH

FIGURE 10

CAVE ENTRANCE

CAVE AREA PHOTOGRAPHED 2 FEB 68

FIGURE 11

important caves, both before and after strikes. All were located in the northwestern corner of the NIAGARA area, the furthest 25 nautical miles from Khe Sanh.117/

One of the most lucrative targets, a primary ammunition and supply area at XD 765227 -- in the Co Roc Mountain area approximately 19 kilometers SSW of Khe Sanh, was reported on 15 February. Covey 673 directed two F-100s against this target at approximately 0425 hours on the 15th, and the strike resulted in three secondary explosions and one secondary fire. This strike was followed at 0848 hours by two A-1Es (Hobo 35) loaded with two BLU 32s, four LAU 59s, two M117s, and four frag bombs each. These Hobos worked the area for almost one hour, and Covey 673 reported that they had destroyed one primary supply area of 150 wooden crates and an ammo cache of 50 to 75 wooden crates. The Hobos also uncovered a 200 meter long trench with crates of ammunition stacked three high. Covey 673 observed the area still exploding and burning after two and one-half hours.118/

The Coveys continued to direct strikes against this target all day on the 15th, recording well over 1,000 secondary explosions and fires.119/ As one FAC reported:

> *"This area is an extremely lucrative target that continues to grow in size and importance as more bombs open up and uncover more and more supply areas and ammo caches. Hobo 35 and Warpaint 300 (2 A-4s) have opened up extensive underground*

> *trenches 200 meters long with hundreds of crates of ammo. This appears to be a major portion of supply area. All areas struck with exception of two caves and 200 meter camouflaged trenches. Recommend Sky Spot throughout evening to prevent relocation of supplies. FAC received light SA fire from three kilometers south of target."*

At 0200 hours on the following morning, Covey 673 VR'd this same area for ammunition and supply caches, and sighted signs of activity during the night. The previously reported trench filled with crates of ammunition had been partly emptied; the removed crates had been emptied and left in the area. However, there were still four large caches in the trench ranging "from 50 crates and up", about 2 x 2 feet and 3 x 9 feet in size. There were also a great number of crates and bags of rice stored above ground. Between 0259 and 0541 hours on the 16th, Covey 673 directed several more flights in against this target, reporting positive results. Since this target could well have been a major staging area for future attacks against Khe Sanh, the FAC strongly urged positive action be taken immediately to deny these supplies to the enemy. He suggested the following plans: 120/

- Helicopter-landing a reaction force to discover the extent of storage, plant demolition, and extract. FAC had received negative ground fire and had seen no active enemy defenses in the area.

- Continuous day bombing by A-1E with napalm. Easily the best results had been achieved by this FAC with A-1E pinpoint placing of napalm and strafe. This is considered to be especially important where targets are in a confined area and require direct hit to destroy.

Extensive ARC LIGHT for area coverage. FAC believed that an aggressive combination of these possible solutions could deny these supplies to the enemy.

The Hillsboro ABCCC mission report for 16 February commented: "I would like to commend Covey 673 for the outstanding FAC job he has done the last three days. It is the best I have seen in the 20 months I have flown Hillsboro. Stream of strikes set up to cover area... to continue through the night." 121/

With the 7AF TACC controlling the effort through the ABCCC, tactical air was able to respond more rapidly to targets acquired. Flights could be readily diverted from fragged targets to strike immediately under FAC control as required. For instance, hot item targets, which were by definition an immediate threat and transitory, when developed by the Intelligence Task Force were passed immediately to the TACC. In turn, the TACC would make direct contact with the ABCCC to place an immediate strike on the target. 122/

The single greatest hindrance to target acquisition and tactical response in the NIAGARA area was the northeast monsoon, for which the enemy had planned to his advantage. During January, February, and part of March, weather in NIAGARA was extremely bad, restricting visual acquisition of targets and ordnance delivery. Much of the time, heavy clouds engulfed the mountain peaks throughout the area, while fog hugged the valley floors around Khe Sanh. Because of this, a high percentage of tactical strikes had to be directed into the target area by MSQ or

Marine TPQ ground directed radar bombing units. [123]

During the first 29 days, before the monsoon peak had passed, a daily average of 65.2 percent of all ABCCC controlled NIAGARA strikes were directed by these Combat Skyspot radar systems. It is logical to assume that an equally high number of other tactical air strikes (controlled by other agencies during the early part of NIAGARA) were flown into the area under ground radar direction. A Marine TPQ was actually positioned at the Khe Sanh Base Camp, and according to Covey FACs who observed strikes directed by this unit, it was highly accurate in directing strikes in its own defense--more so than units positioned further away. [124]

The Coveys also worked with the fighters making strikes under Skyspot direction, and often assisted by reporting results and target adjustments to the fighters. At times, when not forewarned of Skyspot strikes in the area, the Coveys have found themselves in the unenviable position of ordnance being expended over the area in which they were flying. [125]

One of the 7AF liaison officers, who was also a Covey FAC, at Khe Sanh considered the TPQ located there to be one of the primary weapons systems for defense of the base. It was also considered to be a primary target for enemy artillery being applied against Khe Sanh. The liaison officer noted that if a major assault against the base had been made, this TPQ could "effectively be used against enemy forces in close proximity," while the effectiveness of units located further away would be questionable. He made the suggestion that a back-up TPQ be provided at Khe Sanh, since the enemy could well score a direct hit against the single unit. Although this system was out of commission for periods of short duration, it was fortunately not demolished by incoming fire. 126/

Another factor which had an impact on effective application of tactical strikes was obvious: ordnance on occasion being incompatible to terrain or targets being struck. This, of course, is always a primary consideration in tactical air application; however, ordnance selection considerations were compounded in NIAGARA due to the great amount of airpower being applied in the area, and the great variety of tactical target situations which could develop. A good example of ordnance incompatibility was reported in the Lang Vei attack, when immediately available tactical aircraft were armed with heavy bombs, and the ground situation precluded the effective application of such ordnance. Problems in ordnance selection were more prevalent during the first few weeks of NIAGARA, when certain coordination and control conditions adversely affected tactical planning. This will be discussed more fully under "Coordination and Control".

By late February, the 7AF Director of Combat Operations advised all tactical units that "it is becoming increasingly imperative" that the pressure on enemy forces and the effectiveness of strikes "be maximized". 127/ Not only had the pressure against Khe Sanh become

more intense, but the enemy had actually burrowed in around the Khe
Sanh perimeter. One trench was discovered extending beneath the base
defense wire, and it was estimated that the enemy might attempt to
tunnel beneath the defensive positions and plant explosives. A III
MAF report noted:[128/]

> "On 25 February, a 3rd Mar Div AO observed a trench
> extending due north to within 50 meters of the Khe
> Sanh Combat Base perimeter. This new trench is an
> extension of the trench network reported in earlier
> message. This represents approximately 700 meter
> extension in less than 24 hours. New trench is
> reported to be two foot wide, approximately four
> foot deep and terminates in a trench approximately
> 50 meters long running parallel to Khe Sanh wire.
> Another trench was observed, and the AO received
> intense automatic weapons fire from trenches and
> surrounding area."

The 7AF Commander continued to place emphasis on the effective application of tactical airpower against targets developed in the Khe Sanh area. The around-the-clock weight of effort was sustained against these targets, and a special office had been established within the TACC to closely monitor the NIAGARA effort, and keep the commander and his staff posted. Also, a separate frag team had been formed to develop the NIAGARA frag order -- to more effectively apply the total weight of effort.[129/]
In accordance with this command emphasis, 7AF tactical units were given the following directions on 26 February:

> "All strike pilots and FACs will be briefed prior to
> next flight on the criticality of the ground situation
> and the urgency of using every means to press home the

ENEMY TRENCHWORK AROUND KHE SANH - 28 FEB 68

FIGURE 12

> *attack. Specifically, release altitudes for dive deliveries must be reduced to minimums to improve accuracy in destroying pin point targets and effecting road interdictions. Upon completion of dive deliveries, maximum time, within fuel limitations, will be spent on armed reconnaissance of routes and key LOCs in the target area with first priority on Route 9 and Route 922... The areas along Route 9 and 922 are loaded with supplies cached on either side of the road and troops have also been seen in these areas. If no specific targets are found the FACs will direct flights to expend 20-mm in strafing runs along the sides of the roads from the road bed to 50 to 100 yards out.*
>
> *Any areas from which secondary explosions or fires are observed will be struck by follow-on flights. FACs are directed to be especially alert for tanks, trucks and armored vehicles parked close to roads and rivers and for POL drums and other supply caches.*
>
> *It is imperative that Route 9 from Tchepone to Khe Sanh be maintained unserviceable with maximum interdiction effort. F-105s diverted from Alpha Package will be carrying 1/3 time delay bombs and will be given priority for interdiction strikes along Route 9.*
>
> *To assist intelligence gathering efforts, maximum use will be made of gun cameras, KA 71 and strike cameras with film forwarded through intelligence channels to 7AF DI.*
>
> *The urgency of immediate increased pressure on the enemy forces is of the highest priority and every effort is directed to maximize the effectiveness of our air resources."*

Several tactical strikes in immediate support of Khe Sanh near the end of February were reported to be very productive. Strikes on 25 February were a good example. Just before noon on the 25th, the ABCCC reported that Khe Sanh was under heavy fire from rockets and mortars. Although the NIAGARA area was "generally unworkable" except by Combat Skyspot during this period, portions of the western area opened for short periods at midday for visual strikes. Khe Sanh was in this western portion, and the Covey FACs spotted seven rocket and mortar positions which were directing fire against the base. A-1s with soft ordnance were immediately diverted to strike these targets.[131/] The Coveys also directed jets in against the guns, and the combined strikes silenced them. All seven positions were reported destroyed or damaged.[132/]

Every break in the weather was exploited to conduct visual strikes against the enemy forces immediately threatening Khe Sanh. On the previous day, the 24th, the weather had broken around Khe Sanh during the afternoon, and Hillsboro reported:[133/]

> *"Flights with napalm and high drags were scrambled throughout the afternoon against troop concentrations and gun emplacements in the Khe Sanh area..."*

While continuing to press attacks against active targets in the vicinity of Khe Sanh at every opportunity, tactical fighters also continued to interdict enemy logistical movement into the area. Heavy traffic continued to be noted on all routes and trails in all of the NIAGARA area, the Laotian corridors, and Route Package I. The ABCCCs constantly reported that the FACs were involved with strikes against truck parks and moving vehicles. For instance, on 23 February, the "Alleycat" ABCCC reported that strikes in Route Package I had destroyed 43 trucks and two probably destroyed. These strikes also produced 36 secondary explosions and 25 fires.[134/]

One example in the NIAGARA area occurred on 24 February. After the TACC briefed the "Hillsboro" ABCCC on a truck park discovered by NIAGARA photographic reconnaissance taken on 17 January, Covey 671 checked on one of the coordinates, XC808843, and reported it to be a very likely area. After two flights worked the target, Covey 671 reported the largest bunker he had ever seen. A total of six flights produced six secondary explosions and one bunker destroyed. 135/ Earlier, on 22 February, the Coveys had directed strikes against numerous trucks, and reported twelve were destroyed. They also reported nine secondary explosions and 14 fires. 136/

"Nail" FACs from Nakhon Phanom working the STEEL TIGER interdiction area near NIAGARA also continuously sighted trucks which were probably supporting the enemy around Khe Sanh. In one instance, on 24 February, Nail 47 sighted a truck towing a howitzer. The truck was moving east toward Khe Sanh with the weapon. Both the truck and the howitzer were destroyed by two tactical flights. 137/

Covey FAC reports indicated that despite the continuous interdiction effort, the enemy continued to move, often over what were considered to be impassable trails. Roads were under constant repair. For example, in late February, Coveys 123 and 135 reported on the condition of Route 9: 138/

> "VR'd Route 9 between Tchepone and Khe Sanh. Route is being used by both trucks and tracked vehicles. Tread tracks observed entire length of Route VR'd. Repair

61

> work is being done over the entire length of this road. Culverts are being constructed to replace destroyed bridges and fords. Road cuts and ford cuts are apparently ineffective along this route at this time as they are all being bypassed or repaired immediately."

On the same day, Covey 658 reported on enemy road repair: 139/

> "Observed 100 meters of road 15 ft wide running north to south through a deep depression with heavy foliage along both sides. One week ago only ten meters of this road was observed."

Seeding the roads with MK36 mines was also accomplished. The overall effect of these missions was considered to be favorable; however, there were occasions when a mission proved ineffective. One FAC reported one instance in which the mines were observed "going off right after seeding took place". This caused a chain reaction setting off several others. He suggested that the MK36 be used on Route 9 and fords in the evening hours. In the event of similar occurrence, disruption of night traffic might be effected even though the seeding mission failed. 140/

While pressing the attack against the enemy, the FACs and fighters faced very heavy and accurate enemy ground fire. One FAC reported on his experience during the first few weeks of the operation: 141/

> "We have had a difficult time determining any kind of pattern of enemy fire. Small arms in some areas is very intense. Generally, they won't open up with small arms unless you have found something, or they really have something they want to protect. One experience really caught me off guard. I was a few miles from

> *Target 10, which had been previously identified as a pretty heavy triple A threat area. Being new at the time, I wasn't familiar with it. They really opened up on me, before I spotted anything. I applied the general tactic, which is to turn a lot and get as close to the ground as possible, and departed the area.*
>
> *We came back in later on a VR flight, about two miles from the hot area, and again they started opening up on us. Real heavy fire; they chased us around the sky for a long time. We finally located the guns and determined that there were ten or twelve 37mm guns sitting out around Target 10, all revetted."*

Judging from past combat experience, weapons discipline was a basic characteristic of seasoned enemy forces in Vietnam. Normal FAC experience was that seasoned enemy troops would not open fire on aircraft until certain of FAC detection, i.e. FAC aircraft loitering over the target for an extended period or actually directing fighters to the target. 142/ In Operation NIAGARA, however, FACs on more than one occasion found themselves being fired upon, without having detected enemy positions. This probably resulted from the large number of enemy forces in the area and the continuous air activity. In view of the fact that all forces in the area were NVA soldiers, it would appear logical that they were well trained troops, if not seasoned veterans. They were certainly well armed; practically every enemy position and vehicle convoy had anti-aircraft fire support. This is reflected in the following excerpts from FAC reports during one four day period in late February: 144/

> . Covey received 23-mm fire from four positions north of target 674. The fire was very accurate from all four positions. FAC suggests guns are radar controlled

because fire from all positions converged into close proximity of FAC. FAC was at 6500 ft AGL and the rounds were bursting both above and below the aircraft. The line of fire from positions was straight at the aircraft and came very close to hitting. The night was very dark with no moon and aircraft did not have lights on and still fire was very accurate. It would be impossible to come this close to hitting the aircraft by shooting at a sound at 6500 ft AGL.

FAC received heavy 37-mm fire from one position west of target 713 and eight to ten positions approximately 1000 meters south of target 713. FAC received approximately 500 rounds from one position. 37-mm was extremely accurate. Weapon probably centrally controlled.

FACs received 250-300 rounds, inaccurate fire bursting at 10,000-14,000 feet from 10 37-mm positions. FAC recommends suppressor fighter aircraft be made available both night and day for the Target 4107 and 713 interdiction points. Intense 37-mm fire from these points virtually makes it impossible to put in strike aircraft. Hard ordnance is almost useless at night. Recommend CBU-24 and CBU-29.

VR'd Route 96 from D-39 to D-89. Sighted with Starlight scope four trucks going north. While following the trucks, FACs received 50-cal fire from a position just north of the trucks. FAC suspects the AA weapon was mounted on a truck as the fire seemed to come from the road. While FAC was evading the AA fire, he sighted three vehicles moving south. While watching these trucks, FAC received 23-mm fire from the vicinity of target 621. While evading this fire, FAC also drew fire from a 23-mm position in the vicinity of target 674.

Coveys 673 and 642 sighted numerous fires in vicinity of road throughout target area. Trucks were picked up moving through these fires. FAC had difficulty with situation and believes fires are being used to obstruct observation of area for vehicle movement. FAC recommends heavy ordnance on interdiction points in target 4107 and target 713 area. Target 713 has many gun positions defending this area making it almost non-permissive for FAC type aircraft.

The enemy threat in the NIAGARA area did not appear to wane by the end of February; however, his one major advantage--the northeast monsoon--was on the decline. Although there would still be days of inclement weather in March, there would also be more breaks in the weather--making the enemy more vulnerable to pin-point targeting and visual expenditure by tactical fighters. At this point, the 7AF Commander reported to COMUSMACV: 145/

> *"In the first thirty-nine days of Operation NIAGARA, U.S. Air Forces--Tactical, Naval, Marine and Strategic--have dropped fifty-three thousand four hundred tons of ordnance in support of the defense of Quang Tri Province...*
>
> *"This effort has produced more than two thousand five hundred secondary explosions, nearly one thousand secondary fires, and has destroyed or damaged one thousand structures and bunkers. More than one hundred trucks have been destroyed, and unknown number of enemy soldiers have been killed or wounded. Captured documents and prisoners continue to reflect postponement of scheduled operations and destruction of LOCs. These results, impressive as they are, reflect the achievement of slightly more than one-half of the thirteen thousand three hundred effective strike sorties that were flown between 22 January and 29 February. The damage caused by the remainder, forced by*

> *poor weather to release munitions under radar
> control, cannot be assessed directly. The air
> support so far rendered to land forces in Operation
> NIAGARA is unprecedented in the history of aerial
> warfare. Although these operations appear to
> have contributed much to thwarting the enemy's
> plans, they should not be looked upon as an ef-
> fective substitute for those ancillary ground
> actions which alone can frustrate the enemy's
> effort to tunnel into and under the Khe Sanh base."*

ARC LIGHT Responsiveness

As previously noted, the destructive bombing capability of the B-52 ARC LIGHT force was a key element in the sustained NIAGARA effort. MACV targeting for the B-52s and actual strike operations were underway prior to the beginning of sustained tactical strikes on 22 January. According to MACV officials, established procedures prior to NIAGARA had been tailored to strike relatively stable, well-known targets. With the commencement of NIAGARA, the requirement was for rapid response of the B-52s to targets as they were developed. To accomplish this rapid response capability, the area of interest was overlaid with a system of preplanned grids with each grid comparable to the area covered by a B-52 mission. This provided a means for rapid coordination between the ground and the air officials in the preparation and strike of selected targets. It also provided the capability to divert the B-52 strike aircraft within three hours of bomb release. 146/

The Intelligence Control Center generated targets 24 hours a day, as ground units and specialized sensors fed in new data. Tactical air responded on short notice, dropping under radar control if weather or darkness precluded visual attack. New procedures were devised under the nickname BUGLE NOTE which enabled the B-52s to respond with similar flexibility. The NIAGARA area was overlaid by a grid system in which each "box" represented a 1 x 2 kilometer target, an area that could be effectively covered by one cell of B-52s. Under the new concept, every one and one half hours, a cell of three B-52 aircraft would arrive at a predesignated pre-IP to be picked up by MSQ and directed to one of a series of IPs and then to a specific target. The target could be changed each one and one half hours or could be kept the same for each arriving force until required at another aiming point. With regard to B-52 targeting, SAC explained: [147/]

> "To further simplify mission planning and stabilize reaction, secondary/alternate targets would preferably be located in the Kontum/Dak To area. These targets must be capable of supporting the entire effort. Once fragged, the alternate/secondary target must remain in effect."

SAC explained that the B-52s would be expending ordnance on a target in the area of concern every one and one half hours. These TOTs could be varied to as low as one hour spread or increased to two hours as necessary to preclude establishing a TOT pattern for the enemy. The timing of this operation was described as follows: [148/]

> "A cell of three B-52s would take off from Andersen every three hours and proceed to its MSQ pick up point pre-IP and then through IP to target arriving as an example at 1200Z, 1500Z, 1800Z, etc. Every three hours a cell of three aircraft would take off from U-Tapao and proceed to its assigned MSQ pick up point pre-IP and through IP to target arriving there at 1300Z, 1630Z, 1930Z, etc."

Certain limitations are inherent in an operation of this type. SAC listed the following: (1) MSQ must have a target for a cell to drop every one and one half hours, (2) No other ARC LIGHT targets could be attacked during the period this emergency operation is in progress, i.e. 48 sorties per day during emergency in I Corps area, (3) and, for strikes in the SAM Watch Zone, TINY TIM (EB-66s) would be required.[149/] CINCPAC cautioned that the cyclic type of operation conducted under BUGLE NOTE would permit the enemy to arrive at rather accurate estimates of the time the B-52s would be in the vulnerable area. Thus, the enemy would have an increased potential to exploit his capability to launch a MIG attack against B-52s in northernmost I Corps. "All forces need to be particularly alert to this new dimension of the threat," CINCPAC advised.[150/]

SAC also advised that it was prepared to support ARC LIGHT with alternately six or nine sorties per day from the Port Bow (Korea Contingency) resources located at Kadena AB, Okinawa "subject to JCS approval and availability of weapons".[151/] COMUSMACV concurred fully with the SAC proposal, and requested CINCPAC approval. Regarding the use of Kadena resources, COMUSMACV requested two additional strikes of six aircraft per day, if available and approved. These would be in addition to the 48, and would be utilized below the 14 degree parallel. COMUSMACV made the following points relative to BUGLE NOTE Implementation:[152/]

> Secondary targets when required would be designated and submitted twelve hours prior to effective time.

- TINY TIM support would consist of EB-66 coverage in the SAC designated SAM Watch Zone.

- Iron Hand would be provided whenever the target route penetrated a known or suspected SAM ring.

- The use of BLU munitions was considered and not deemed feasible for the operation due to troop clearance requirements and lack of flexibility to use secondary/alternate targets. However, BLU munitions would be requested on specific targets when they could be used to advantage.

CINCPAC approval was obtained, and the BUGLE NOTE concept was implemented on 15 February, along with the sortie increase through use of the Kadena B-52s. In NIAGARA, this meant around-the-clock B-52 operations -- 16 missions per day with three aircraft each over the target every one and one-half hours. Shortly after implementation of this improved concept in NIAGARA, COMUSMACV requested that a BUGLE NOTE capability be developed for certain other key target zones in South Vietnam. Five days after NIAGARA terminated, the Chief, SAC ADVON, at Hq 7AF reported on BUGLE NOTE developments to that time:[153/]

> "... 3AD supplies ten six ship sorties a day to pre-determined IP gates and SAC/ADVON/TACPAL provides target information to the MSQ sites. A southern and central BUGLE NOTE capability has also been developed and MACV now has an ARC LIGHT reaction capability (by target selection or change) of three hours. In the few areas not covered by BUGLE NOTE IPs, the usual 24 hours in advance preplanned missions will be used. The sortie rate and this target change capability down to within three hours of TOT has resulted in elimination of the Quick Run Alert Force.

> *ADVON is now fulfilling the original Terms of Reference in functioning as the operational planning agency. We select all TOTs, weaponeer the target, recommend axis of attack and base to provide the strike for preplanned missions. All of the BUGLE NOTE planning from pre-IP through target is the sole responsibility of ADVON. The relationship with MACV is excellent and their actions are now primarily concerned with target evaluation and selection..."*

Another significant development concerned a relaxation of the rules for B-52 strikes. Prior to NIAGARA the B-52s were restricted from expending their ordnance to within three kilometers of friendly positions. On 13 February, COMUSMACV advised CINCPAC that the tactical situation at Khe Sanh and in other areas of Quang Tri, such as Con Thien and Camp Carroll, "may require that full defensive fires be brought into close proximity of defensive positions". He recommended that the 3 kilometer clearance from friendly combatants be rescinded, and that this clearance be determined on the basis of the tactical situation, by the tactical commander, as approved by Hq MACV. 154/ The clearance limitation was subsequently relaxed to one kilometer from friendly combatants. 155/

Discussion of the B-52 effectiveness in the NIAGARA area will be covered in the operational summary. Prisoner and captured document information relative to B-52 strikes will also be presented in that section; however, it seems appropriate to conclude this section of the study with the comments of one Marine ground commander relative to the results of one B-52 strike of 9 February. On this date, this officer's unit received the support of two ARC LIGHT strikes, one at 1700 hours and one at 1750. He reported: 156/

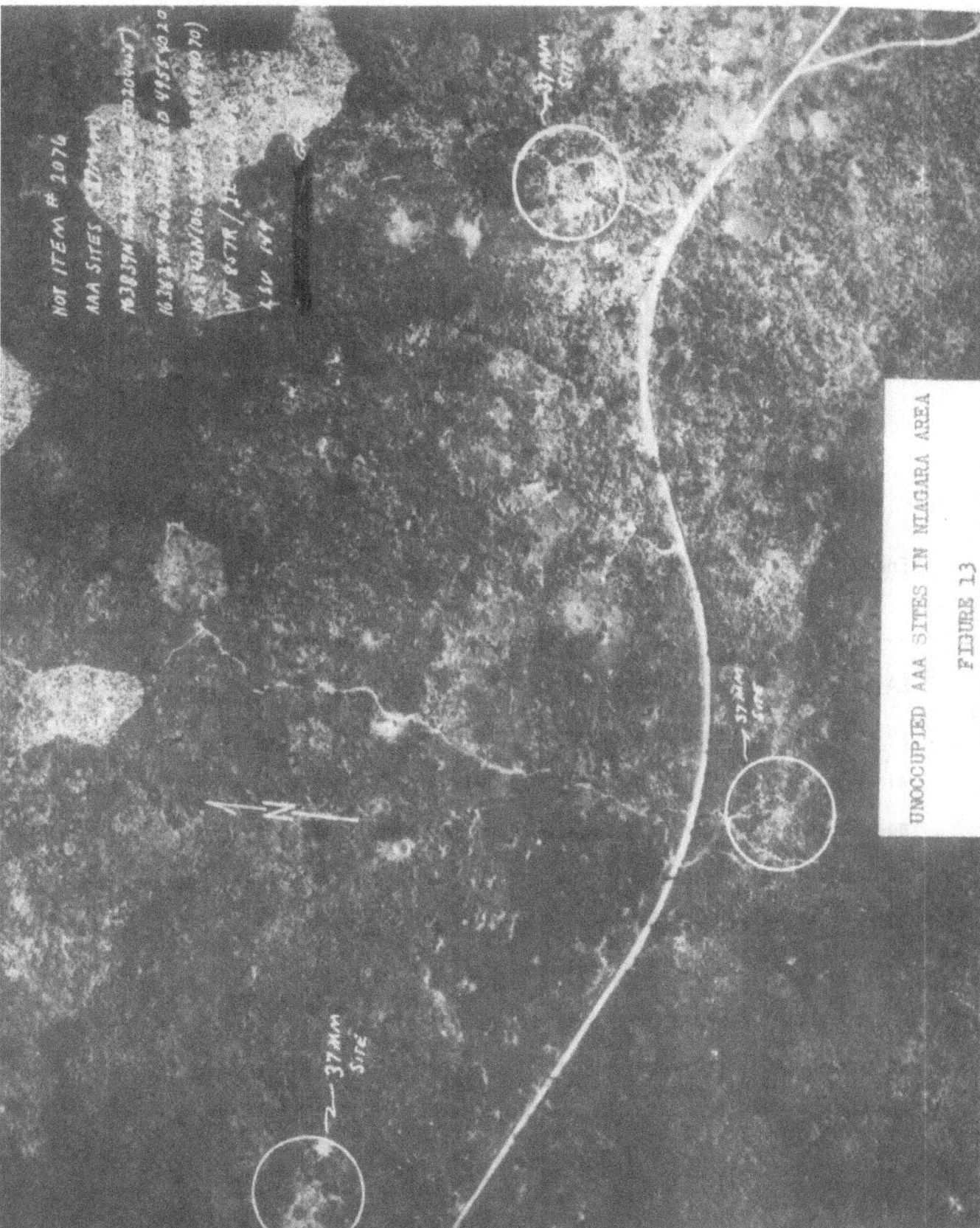

UNOCCUPIED AAA SITES IN NIAGARA AREA

FIGURE 13

> "*All in the area were awed at the devastating accuracy and destruction displayed by your pilots and weaponry. For the past two weeks enemy activity in and around the target has been such that our ground operations have been exposed to continual harassment. It is my belief that today these enemy forces were struck a blow so severe as to render them ineffective for an appreciable period.*
>
> *"A large number of NVA troops were observed actually running from the bombed zone following the first strike. They seemed oblivious to anything but putting distance between themselves and the oncoming bombs. Consequently, all were travelling in the same direction and at the same speed presenting a very tight, compact target. Observers witnessed one bomb of the second strike score a direct hit on the group which, needless to relate, utterly disappeared."*

Enemy Counter Air Activities

As previously mentioned, the enemy made provisions for an active AA defense of key areas around Khe Sanh. 7AF Intelligence officials reported that in scope and firepower they were totally inadequate. Almost all were automatic weapons or small arms. The largest caliber AA threat against tactical aircraft proved to be the 37mm AA gun, frequently reported but never clearly photographed during NIAGARA. Every identified 37mm site was struck until its destruction or abandonment could be confirmed by photography. Smaller AA/AW positions were attacked visually whenever they posed a threat to the air mission. Over 300 gun positions were reported destroyed (by either aircrew observation or photo BDA) out of more than 600 struck during NIAGARA. 157/

Extensive steps were taken to suppress ground fire in the approach and egress lanes to the Khe Sanh airstrip. The ground track of aircraft arriving and departing Khe Sanh was plotted from the point where an incoming flight would penetrate 3500' AGL to the point where outbound aircraft would regain that altitude. From that center line a lateral offset was made equivalent to the slant range of the 37-mm AA weapon against the flight path. This established approach and withdrawal lanes within which the active flak suppression operation was conducted. Transports entered, normally from the east. FAC aircraft flew off either wing-tip to spot AA positions and direct strikes, with escort fighters in trail. All signs of AA fire -- flashes or puffs of smoke -- were immediately engaged. As an additional aid, other fighters laid smoke parallel to the runway center line along the approach and departure routes.[158/]

The flak suppression effort was extensive and ultimately effective. Although roughly two-thirds of the tonnage delivered during NIAGARA was air-dropped, landings were made at Khe Sanh on all but eight of the 70 days of the operation. All in all, 56 aircraft were hit and three downed representing 0.2 per cent of the total sorties flown. An additional C-123 was destroyed on the ground.[159/]

Against the B-52s, the enemy could protect himself as he had through the years along the Ho Chi Minh Trail by concealment, dispersal and constant movement. However, his concentration on a point objective limited movement and dispersal, and the intensive NIAGARA targeting effort destroyed his concealment. A credible SAM threat in NIAGARA might have inhibited ARC LIGHT operations, but there is no evidence the enemy attempted to introduce one. Ten days prior to NIAGARA, he fired four SAMs at a formation of B-52s over the central DMZ (YD087844-1702N/10655E), and intelligence carried a SAM threat in this general area throughout the NIAGARA period, but no more firings were observed until 25 May, almost two months after NIAGARA ended. 160/

Tactical Airlift at Khe Sanh

From the time the decision was made to hold Khe Sanh, its tenability became almost solely dependent upon airpower. This was true, whether the enemy really looked upon the besieged base camp as a major objective, or whether they merely considered it a point of diversion for other alternatives. The primary defense of Khe Sanh was the sustained tactical strike and B-52 effort -- without which the base could well have fallen.

The 6,000-man U.S. Marine and ARVN force at Khe Sanh was equally dependent upon airlift for its tenability. With the enemy occupying the high ground around it, and its ground supply routes severed, Khe Sanh would have become isolated had it not been for air resupply.

Although the III MAF had an organic airlift capability, it was not within their capability to assume a resupply role of the magnitude required at Khe Sanh. Thus, it became largely dependent upon the 834th Air Division to keep the base resupplied and to evacuate the wounded.

By the time the ground resupply routes had been reopened almost three months later, the 834th AD had delivered over 12,400 tons of supplies to the forces at Khe Sanh. Of this effort, 8,120 tons were delivered by airdrop, and 4,310 by air landing under extremely hazardous conditions.[161]

Prior to mid-February, enemy bombardment at Khe Sanh had become so accurate and intense that all aircraft landing at the airstrip had become prime enemy targets. "We have let the NVA get so close that he can put .50-caliber fire on the center line one half mile from final," one pilot commented on 19 February. No sooner would aircraft land, than incoming mortar, rocket, and artillery fire would begin. A Covey FAC who often landed at Khe Sanh made the following observations:[162]

> "Enemy weaponry has been moved up now (mid-February) to the point where we are being bombarded by high-angle short distance trajectory, rather than low-angle long distance trajectory. For example, there is a hole just off the runway at Khe Sanh that is quite unlike those made during January. The ones on 21 January were long gouges with little depth. There is a hole up there today that is a real crater. That round went straight up and came straight down. We still land there, but we won't land when there is a C-123 or C-130 there because they are a magnet for this heavy bombardment."

In view of the extremely hazardous ground situation and monsoon weather conditions, 834th AD officials advised the III MAF that air drop methods would have to supplement ground offloadings if the required tonnages were to be delivered at Khe Sanh. Three air drop methods would be used: (1) Ground Proximity Extraction System (GPES), (2) Container

C-130 AIR DROP AT KHE SANH

FIGURE 14

SUPPLIES LANDING IN DROP ZONE

FIGURE 15

C-130 PREPARES FOR DEPARTURE FROM KHE SANH. SMOKE RISES FROM A LINE OF DEFENSIVE FIRE LAID DOWN BY 7AF AND NAVY STRIKE AIRCRAFT.

FIGURE 16

Delivery System (CDS), and (3) Low Altitude Parachute Extraction System (LAPES). Navigational techniques and problems associated with these air drops will be discussed under "Coordination and Control".[163]

At first, the Marines were reluctant to agree that air drops represented the optimum means of delivery under the existing conditions. There were certain drawbacks, from the ground point of view. For instance, there was not sufficient room within the defense perimeter, and drops had to be made outside the "secure" area. This required additional security measures, and presented potential problems in recovery. One report also said that the Marine commanders were concerned that a slackening off in aircraft landings would adversely affect troop morale.[164] Perhaps the opposite was the case, in view of the fact that a definite rise in enemy shelling occurred with aircraft landings.

Also, since the drop zone was outside the base perimeter, it was unguarded overnight, thus requiring sweep operations each morning to secure the area for drops. The drop zone also had to be cleared of supplies prior to withdrawal in the evening. This resulted in a compressed daily time period for resupply drops.[165] Although most drops were successful, another problem arose when some drops went astray and could not be recovered prior to nightfall. These had to be destroyed to prevent enemy capture.[166]

Recovery time by the Marines, of course, was directly proportionate to the location of the drop. Pallets located within the drop zone were quickly recovered. The Marines reported that the average time required to clear one drop was 45 minutes if all pallets were in the drop zone. Pallets outside the drop zone resulted in several additional hours for recovery.[167/]

Although initially reluctant, the Marine commanders were soon convinced of the reliability of the 834th AD effort. A III MAF message to the 7AF Commander on 26 February said:[168/]

> *"Accuracy of drops has shown daily improvement, attesting to professional competence of air crews, GCA personnel and mission planners. Every effort being made to increase drop zone recovery capability and protect radars, in order to attain goal of 235 short tons daily. Progress hampered by enemy action and adverse weather."*

By using the air drop modes, along with the navigational techniques discussed in the next section of this study, the 834th AD was able to keep Khe Sanh amply supplied under extremely adverse conditions. Mission Commander reports and other official documents revealed the following information which might enhance future planning of similar operations:[169/]

- The 7AF Commander directed that fighter aircraft would escort all tactical airlift aircraft into Khe Sanh. Thus, air logistics operations received support from strike aircraft expending smoke, napalm, and diverse hard ordnance throughout the approach, ground-handling and take-off phases.

- C-130s and C-123s provided the major effort, with the C-130s being the prime deliverer. A few C-7A sorties were flown, but it was determined that the relatively small capacity of this aircraft was insufficient for the effort and risk involved, and its use was discontinued.

For coordination purposes, the Air Force sent 7-10 man airlift teams to Khe Sanh, for 10-14 days each. These teams controlled maintenance, offloading, onloading, and all supply aircraft in the area. They also marked the drop zones, coordinated deliveries, and served as back-up air traffic controllers with their own communications equipment.

Supply activities were limited to daylight hours, because night operations would present the enemy with too easily distinguishable targets. Also, the supply drop zone was much too vulnerable for night operations.

Aerial delivery did not completely eliminate the risks to aircraft. By monitoring ground to air transmissions, the enemy often discovered arrival times and were able to direct fire as aircraft began their runs.

Optimum airlift planning and response requires early determination of firm supply requirements in terms of tonnage by the ground commander. Firm requirements at Khe Sanh were not provided to 834th Air Division planners until two weeks after the airlift effort began.

Coordination and Control

In the planning and execution phases of Operation NIAGARA, both COMUSMACV and the 7AF Commander stressed close coordination between participating forces and optimum control of weapon systems being employed. In view of the great amount and variety of air and ground weaponry being employed in this sustained operation, the basic elements of coordination and control required more attention than they would under ordinary operational circumstances. From the Air Commander's point of view, the objective was to provide optimum airpower within the boundaries established by the tactical situation and the resources available to him -- while assuring maximum conditions of safety and effectiveness for participating air forces. A major consideration, of course, was that this not be accomplished at the expense of other tactical situations which were developing throughout the theatre tactical zones.

The responsibility for optimum application of air resources in Operation NIAGARA rested clearly with the 7AF Commander, as directed by COMUSMACV. In accordance with COMUSMACV directive, the 7AF Commander, in his role as Deputy COMUSMACV for air operations, would "coordinate and direct the employment of the tactical air, Marine air, diverted air strikes from out of country air operations, and such Naval air that may be requested." B-52 operations were to be coordinated through him. One exception with regard to the control of tactical air was made. Although III MAF was directed to make available to 7AF all tactical strike sorties not required for direct air support of Marine units, III MAF was authorized to retain control of the effort in direct support of its own units.[170/] This exception left the matter of control of Marine air assets open to interpretation at the beginning of NIAGARA operations, with the end result being a negative impact on air planning and application of air resources in the area of concern during the first few weeks.

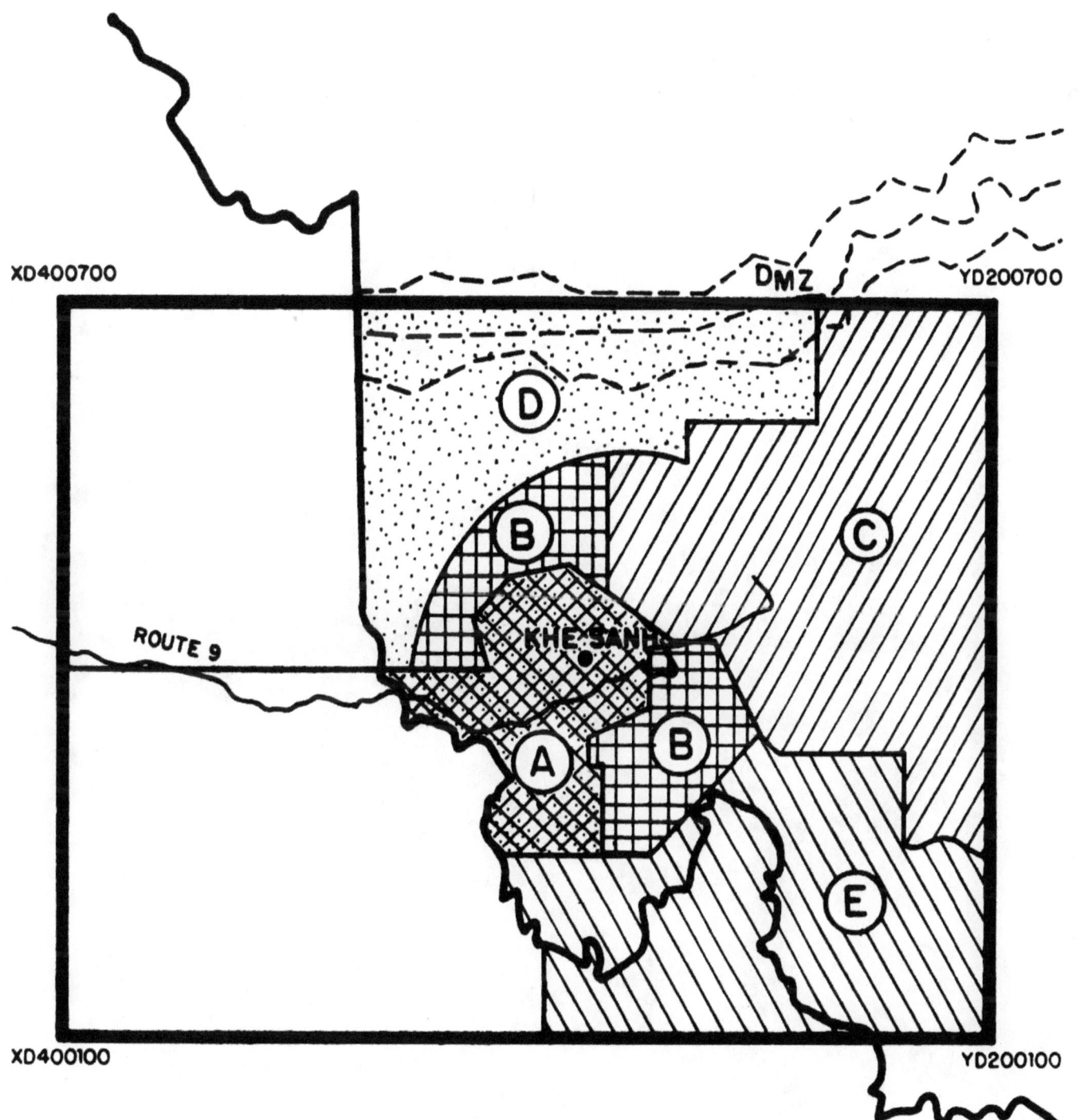

FIGURE 17

III MAF's interpretation of command and control for NIAGARA air operations was reflected in a message to 7AF on 24 January. This message defined specific control and coordination zones which were meant "to ensure that the ground commander can employ all supporting arms in his area of responsibility and that air support assets are most effectively utilized." These zones were defined as follows: (Fig. 17) 171/

- Zone Alpha: Restricted fire area coordinated and controlled by the Marine FSCC/DASC at Khe Sanh. Air support was required to be under positive control of FAC, MSQ, or TPQ.

- Zone Bravo: A controlled area in which air strikes and artillery were coordinated by the Marine FSCC/DASC at Khe Sanh. DASC clearance was required for entry. Air strikes could be executed under flight leader control upon approval of FSCC/DASC Khe Sanh.

- Zone Charlie: Restricted fire area coordinated and controlled by Marine FSCC/DASC at Dong Ha. Air support was required to be under positive control of FAC, MSQ, or TPQ.

- Zone Delta and Echo: These were free strike zones. Military targets could be struck as required under flight leader control. CG I Corps granted blanket clearance for strikes of military targets in these areas. There were no known friendly forces operating therein. Air strikes in these zones were under control of 7AF ABCCC. FSCC/DASC Clearance not required.

III MAF further advised that Marine air strike sorties would be conducted primarily in Zones A and B, which were to be controlled by the Marine control agencies at Khe Sanh. 172/ This implied that III MAF would concentrate its total air effort -- including reconnaissance, FAC, strike and targeting -- in one area under its own control. Furthermore, it implied that 7AF could apply its major effort around the III MAF effort, while of course contributing sorties as required in the areas under Marine control. By applying its total effort in one area considered to be "in direct support of its own unit," III MAF's actions were not in consonance with the spirit and intent of the COMUSMACV directive that the 7AF Commander would "coordinate and direct the employment of the tactical air, Marine air, diverted air strikes from out of country air operations, and such Naval air that may be requested." Moreover, it created a confusing control situation whereby airspace congestion and non-availability of aircraft became a common occurrence. Not only did cycling of sorties become a problem, but the planning cycle for target assignments and ordnance selection was severely weakened. 173/

Most of the coordination and control problems encountered in NIAGARA during the first few weeks were directly attributable to the fragmented control arrangements involved in the management of the air program. Thus, this experience brought sharply into focus the long standing requirement for a single manager of tactical air assets in Vietnam. This does not imply that all problems in coordination and control would be immediately resolved by the establishment of centralized control under a single manager. It does mean, however, that coordination between participating forces could be accomplished more smoothly and effectively, and the optimum cycle of air planning and application of resources could be realized. 174/

The sustained weight of effort required in Operation NIAGARA could not be upheld by air resources organic to III MAF. This included both the operations and intelligence capabilities required for successful air application. It was not a question of mere augmentation of III MAF air resources to be applied at the discretion of the III MAF Commander. For an undertaking of this magnitude, the III MAF command and control system could not have effectively absorbed the full input of necessary operations and intelligence assets. Optimum management of the program could be applied only by COMUSMACV through his Deputy Commander for Air and the 7AF TACS which was both doctrinally and functionally designed to manage the total air effort. 175/

COMUSMACV's Deputy Commander for Air -- the 7AF Commander -- had the staff expertise and control system that was required to effectively manage NIAGARA operations. The 7AF TACS was designed to provide the real-time interface between intelligence and operations in the scope required for NIAGARA. Around the clock daily management could assure optimum cycling of sorties into the area of concern -- to include cohesive targeting, tactical response, and traffic control. 176/

Absence of centralized control at the beginning of NIAGARA created a situation whereby two separate air forces were conducting independent air operations in a compressed area of concern. This situation was compounded by the input of a large number of Navy tactical sorties and B-52 sorties into the same area. Problems of coordination between air and artillery were very small in comparison to those involving the different air elements. 7AF had liaison teams collocated with the Marine control agencies at Dong Ha and Khe Sanh to coordinate air matters, and all participating forces had mutual liaison at headquarters' levels. These efforts at coordination, while required, in no way compensated for the lack of centralized management of the tactical air effort.[177/]

As previously mentioned, the lack of centralized planning for the total effort resulted in the inadequate cycling of aircraft. ABCCC mission reports continually emphasized that there were certain periods of air congestion, while FACs continued to report many instances when "no strike aircraft were available" to strike perishable targets. There was an obvious impact on ordnance planning. Ordnance was frequently reported incompatible to targets and terrain being struck. Other factors such as diversions and ordnance requirements for radar-directed strikes also had an impact on this problem; however, much of the inadequacy could be attributed to the lack of centralized management.[178/]

Some specific problems reported by 7AF FACs, who were contributing by far the greatest FAC capability in NIAGARA, and the ABCCC were as follows:[179/]

> ○ ABCCC was not kept informed on the amount of air activity in the "Alpha" and "Bravo" sectors of NIAGARA -- to include FACs. This contributed to a distorted picture of the overall air situation.

- There were isolated instances in which Marine aircraft struck targets outside the "Alpha" and "Bravo" areas without ABCCC knowledge or coordination.

- There were also instances when ARC LIGHT strikes and TPQ and MSQ strikes were made without ABCCC and FAC knowledge. This created a hazardous situation for the FACs who often found themselves flying in the areas where these strikes were being conducted.

- FACs also reported isolated instances of transport aircraft flying through areas where they were directing air strikes in the "Alpha" and "Bravo" zones.

- Two targeting systems in the area created confusion. Frequently one control agency was hindered in assisting the other control agency in conducting strikes against lucrative targets because it was involved with its own targets.

- Further, the application of two targeting systems could conceivably result in a duplication of the strike effort, while allowing the status of other targets to remain active.

- In one instance on 10 February, the Marine control agency would not give the ABCCC strike clearance in the NIAGARA "Charlie" area until the source of target information was provided. The source was required so the Marine control agency could determine its validity and authenticity.

- Although the ABCCC and the Marine TPQ attempted close coordination, there were times that the TPQ was saturated with Marine flights and could not accept Air Force flights for radar control. Some of these flights had to depart the area without expending their ordnance because of bingo fuel.

To improve the command and control situation in NIAGARA, COMUSMACV gave the 7AF Commander full responsibility for the overall air effort for the defense of Khe Sanh. Accordingly, the 7AF Commander advised the CG III MAF and other participants on 13 February that the ABCCC would assume the immediate coordination and handling of the air effort associated with the Khe Sanh area of operations. He advised participants:[180/]

> "Specific instructions and procedures for targets and TOTs will be contained in the daily frag order issued by the 7AF TACC. To achieve success it is expected that the following forces will be committed to this effort: 7AF - 150 sorties; CTF-77 (carrier task force) - 100 sorties; III MAF - 100 sorties; and, SAC ARC LIGHT - 48 sorties. In addition to these strike aircraft there will be numerous FAC aircraft, airlift aircraft, and helicopters operating in the immediate vicinity and/or landing at Khe Sanh. In consideration of effective traffic control and mission accomplishment it is essential that efficient control be established and adhered to by all participants. Targeting and timing details for all aircraft including USN and USMC will be covered in 7AF TACC daily frags.
>
> Procedures: All strike, FAC, support and airlift forces will contact ABCCC prior to entering the area of operations for confirmation of the primary mission and for hand off to the appropriate control agency. Exception: Helicopters operating in the Khe Sanh area will effect safe separation from other traffic and artillery in accordance with existing procedures.
>
> ABCCC will effect direct coordination and control of operations within presently defined NIAGARA area..."

Many of the same coordination and control problems continued to hinder the NIAGARA effort over the next few days. This was primarily the result of delays in the effective integration of Marine air resources into the TACS. CG III MAF took the position that Marine air would adhere to the established control procedures until "modified as a result of concurrence between CG III MAF and Cdr 7AF".[181/] In the meanwhile, the ABCCC reported:[182/]

- **14 Feb**: Marine flights did not check in with Hillsboro ABCCC but worked with Carstairs II (Marine control at Khe Sanh). ARC LIGHTs did not check in. Only fragged information was available. TPQ saturation and target area congestion forced diversion of some aircraft but most fragged targets were struck at some time during the period.

- **15 Feb**: Marine aircraft were not checking in with Moonbeam (night) ABCCC and were going directly to Carstairs control. Resulting congestion required stacking over Channel 85. For approximately one hour Carstairs did not put aircraft on targets requested by Moonbeam.

- **16 Feb**: Hillsboro reported that continuous ARC LIGHT missions prevented MSQs from directing Skyspot strikes the entire time on station. This denial of MSQ-77 facilities (one was out of commission) restricted the ABCCC capability to strike NIAGARA targets and had it not been for the visual capability in western NIAGARA at least a dozen sorties would have had to return to base with their ordnance.

- **17 Feb**: ABCCC had no prior knowledge of ARC LIGHT strikes after midnight which caused a confusion factor when the controlling agency requested target confirmation.

- **17 Feb**: Marine flights still not checking in with ABCCC although AF strikes were applied to Carstairs targets for approximately two hours when he had troops in contact and declared an emergency condition.

- **18 Feb**: Hillsboro controlled AF, Navy and airlift traffic. Marine flights did not check in with Hillsboro, but went direct to Carstairs II.

- **19 Feb**: Moonbeam reported several unsuccessful strike aircraft due to MSQ sites supporting Arc Lights and the Marine TPQ site down due to maintenance.

- **21 Feb**: AF strikes were provided to Carstairs II for lucrative targets in the Khe Sanh area. When arriving on station, ABCCC was advised by Carstairs II that it would not be able to accept AF targets since the TPQ was needed to support resupply missions.

The daily control and coordination problems experienced by the ABCCC continued to reflect the same pattern. ABCCC Commanders strongly recommended that if the ABCCC was to be the prime control for all strikes in the NIAGARA area, the Marine strikes should check in with them prior to working targets. This would facilitate a smoother flow of strike traffic in the area and allow for more efficient control.[183/]
Another recommendation:[184/]

> "*Immediate steps must be taken to review the requirements for MSQ-77 sites to devote their entire efforts toward ARC LIGHT missions. The concept is completely unrealistic for the loss of Carstairs Bravo would have brought all air strikes in the NIAGARA area to a complete standstill except for one ARC LIGHT approximately every 90 minutes. If MSQ-77 sites cannot be made more available for tactical air strikes, then the tactical air sortie rate must be reduced.*"

Later, in early March, many of the coordination and control problems were resolved through integrated planning and a more centrally controlled air effort. Integrated frag teams were established, and the planning and operational cycle for air application became more responsive to tactical requirements. However, many tributaries of control appeared to remain clogged with functional confusion. This was obviously the result of having to make continuing adjustments in the command and control system throughout the execution phase of an air operation, especially one of the force magnitude and time frame constituted by Operation NIAGARA. Of course, under any management concept, operational procedures are continuously reviewed for possible improvement; however, had single management of air assets in Operation NIAGARA been clearly established prior to the execution phase, most potential problems could have been resolved during the operational planning.

A final discussion of control experience in NIAGARA concerns tactical airlift at Khe Sanh. Inclement weather conditions and the hazardous terrain around Khe Sanh required special procedures for all weather delivery of supplies to the besieged Marines. Aircraft supplying Khe Sanh during weather conditions were handed off from Hue Control to the GCA unit at Khe Sanh which was used to guide aircraft to a predetermined point at the approach end of the runway. At that point, because the aircraft came too near to the GCA location for precise direction, a system involving radar reflectors on the runway, the aircraft doppler system, and stopwatch timing was used to guide the aircraft to the proper release point. When the GCA unit was malfunctioning, or when it was knocked out by enemy fire, the Marine TPQ-10 at Khe Sanh supplemented operations. [185/]

Operations Summary

The tactical situation in the NIAGARA area during the month of March was characterized by a continuing high level of enemy activity around Khe Sanh. Incoming artillery, rocket and mortar rounds at Khe Sanh in March were of a greater number than in February. 5,181 rounds of mixed ordnance impacted on the base in March, while 4,710 rounds were received in February. Friendly forces at Khe Sanh suffered 45 KIA and 195 WIA (evacuated) in March. In February, they suffered <u>48 KIA</u> and <u>205 WIA</u> (evacuated). [186/]

Enemy trenchwork around Khe Sanh also continued to expand during March. In one report on the trenches in mid-March, Nail FAC 62 observed:

> *"Trenches from the south are close to the perimeter; many are within 200 meters of the outer fence, and a few go right up to the outer fence. There are now fresh trenches perpendicular to the approach trench forming a 'T' (parallel to the runway). Many foxholes and bunkers are located to the north. South perimeter is covered by trenches and tunnels; foxholes can be seen within the trenches suggesting the presence of personnel on a full time basis."*

Some of the heaviest action at Khe Sanh in March began on the night of the 22nd. Intelligence officials later estimated that the enemy had planned to stage a major assault against Khe Sanh on 22-23 March. Nail 35 who flew in the Khe Sanh area during the daylight hours of 22 March reported "working several flights within 400 meters of the Khe Sanh perimeter." Each bomb that hit a trench produced several secondaries which were believed to be rockets. The FAC also noted "small holes", which he said were not foxholes. These were about 200 feet from the perimeter and dug at an angle so the bottom could only be seen from the west, i.e. over the strip. Nail 35 suggested these might be mortar positions. He also reported no personnel to be seen anywhere near the area and the complete absence of ground fire appeared to confirm this. [188/]

At 1900 hours on the 22nd, Khe Sanh began receiving heavy incoming fire. The volume slacked off for a short period, and then increased in tempo at 2045 hours. III MAF considered this to be a possible pre-assault barrage, and the III MAF Commander passed the following request to 7AF. "Khe Sanh receiving heavy incoming. Request 7th AF be aware of possibility of request for tactical air support at Khe Sanh." By 2400 hours of the 22nd, Khe Sanh had been subjected to a barrage which included 300 artillery rounds, 92 rockets, and 250 mortar rounds -- a total of 642 rounds. Six personnel were killed, and 28 wounded. One ammunition bunker was destroyed, and several artillery pieces were damaged. On the following day, Khe Sanh received another barrage of 636 rounds of mixed ordnance. Thirty-nine friendly personnel were wounded in action, with 17 evacuated.[189]

Tactical air responded with 1,074 sorties between 22 - 24 March in the defense of Khe Sanh, with the largest number being flown on the 23rd -- 438 sorties. The B-52s totalled 138 sorties into the area over the three day period, with 51 of these being flown on 23 March. If an enemy attack was planned, it did not materialize, and the enemy shelling dropped off.[190] The ABCCC reported that on the night of 22 March, Carstairs II had requested specifically that the AC-130 weapon system (Spector 05) be provided for suppression of enemy fire. This request was made at 2200 hours during the heaviest period of enemy shelling. Moonbeam was unable to comply because of AC-130 crew rest, and a Spooky AC-47 was provided instead. No additional air was requested by Carstairs II, and afterward the area was relatively quiet. Moonbeam recommended:

"Spector 05 remains the most effective weapons system against ground troops and movers. Recommend that more of this type aircraft be provided to the theater." [191/]

The stream of tactical air sorties flown in NIAGARA during March remained constant at a daily average of 301. The daily average for the sustained operation between 22 January and 31 March was 300. B-52 sorties increased considerably during March with a daily average of 41, as compared to a daily average of 33 during the first 38 days of NIAGARA operations. Bomb Damage Assessment (BDA) for tactical air showed increased results in March. For instance, there was a daily average of 87 secondary explosions and fires reported in March, compared to a daily average of 65 prior to March. In this comparison, the weather factor must be considered. Although weather was still bad in March, more visual sightings could be made and more visual BDA obtained. [192/]

NIAGARA operations ended on 31 March, with a total of 24,449 tactical air and B-52 sorties having made strikes against the enemy. An additional 1,598 FAC sorties and 1,398 Reconnaissance sorties were flown. Over 100,000 tons of bombs were dropped in the NIAGARA area, and over 100,000 rounds of artillery and mortar ammunition were also fired in support of the combat base at Khe Sanh. [193/] Combat Sky Spot permitted the campaign to proceed without interruption by darkness and bad weather; 62 per cent of NIAGARA air strikes were conducted under Sky Spot control.

Weather precluded accurate BDA of the air effort. Cumulative BDA reported for tactical air strikes in this study was derived from visual sightings and is obviously deflated. FACs had an extremely difficult time making strike assessments because of weather conditions, and post-strike BDA of Sky Spot strikes was negligible. Also, even under good weather conditions, definite BDA was often precluded by smoke, dust and dense foliage. Cumulative BDA gained from visual sightings was reported as follows for tactical air strikes: 4,705 secondary explosions and 1,935 secondary fires; 1,288 KBA; 253 trucks destroyed and 52 damaged; 300 gun positions destroyed and 43 damaged; 891 bunkers destroyed and 99 damaged; 1,061 structures destroyed and 158 damaged; and, nine tanks destroyed and four damaged. [194/]

BDA information on B-52 strikes was also limited. Weather also restricted aerial observation of targets struck by the B-52s. When reconnaissance was possible, much of the damage observed could not be specifically attributed to B-52s because of numerous tactical air strikes and artillery fire in the area. A preliminary MACV study reported the following total number of destroyed/damaged B-52 targets in the Khe Sanh area for the period 15 January to 31 March obtained by visual and photo reconnaissance: [195/]

- Defensive Positions: 274 destroyed and 67 damaged.
- Weapons Positions: 17 destroyed and 8 damaged.
- Lines of Communication: 23 destroyed and 34 damaged.

In addition, SAC aircrews reported approximately 1,362 secondary explosions and 108 secondary fires in the target areas. MACV interpreted:[196/]

> *"It is evident from the above figures that B-52 strikes have destroyed numerous enemy offensive/ defensive positions and disrupted supply and storage areas. Other evidence shows that the enemy has also suffered many casualties to these attacks. Photo reconnaissance of an area near Cam Lo revealed twelve enemy bodies which can be directly attributed to B-52s. According to POW, rallier, and refugee reports, elements of the 304th Division have sustained heavy losses. The attacks were often a surprise to enemy units, and reportedly caused, in addition to KIA, numerous concussion type injuries which required evacuation. An entry in a notebook captured at Khe Sanh reads in part: 'From the beginning until the 60th day (the 60th day of the siege at Khe Sanh) B-52 bombers continually dropped their bombs in this area with ever growing intensity and at any moment of the day. If someone came to visit this place, he might say that this was a storm of bombs and ammunition which eradicated all living creatures and vegetation whatsoever, even those located in caves or in deep underground shelters'.*
>
> *"Desertions apparently resulted from strikes. Reportedly, individuals often took advantage of the confusion immediately after a strike to leave their units. An extract from a captured document, dated 29 Feb 68, states that contingents of Doan 926 suffered 300 desertions while enroute to Khe Sanh. Fear of enemy B-52 raids was given as the main cause for these desertions. The shock, confusion, and destruction brought by B-52s contributed to lowering the morale of the enemy. In one instance, a source said that nearly seventy percent of his unit's rice supply was destroyed by B-52 bombs, causing frustration and hunger. Another source stated that his men were afraid of the strikes because of the supposed high casualties inflicted on the 1st (9th Regt 304 Div).*

> *To lessen the fears of their troops, the NVA undertook a concerted propaganda effort, telling the men not to fear B-52 strikes because bombs had to fall within 3 meters to cause a casualty. Breu refugees were told that they should not fear B-52s, with implications that the NVA had an anti-B-52 device in the Khe Sanh area."*

MACV advised on 20 April that although an accurate and comprehensive estimate of the extent of destruction could not be made at this time, it was almost certain that enemy losses, both personnel and equipment, greatly exceeded those reported.[197/] With data available at the time this study was prepared, an accurate quantitative analysis of the impact of airpower on enemy forces and plans in the NIAGARA area could not be made. Several agencies were engaged in a continuing comprehensive collection and study of pertinent NIAGARA data, and indications were that a final analysis was a long way off. In the final analysis of the impact of airpower in the defense of Khe Sanh, the full scope of the air role must be considered. For instance, the effectiveness of air delivered gravel (anti-personnel mines) on enemy withdrawal routes must be considered. Also, an assessment of 7AF's total interdiction effort during this period and its impact on the Khe Sanh tactical situation would be an essential analytical study ingredient.

Conversely, there would appear to be a need to address the question of what impact a sustained air program of NIAGARA's magnitude might have on the functional response of the 7AF TACS to theatre-wide requirements -- both immediate and long range. This might be correlated with a study to detect any pattern of enemy reaction to predetermined patterns of airpower response in special air programs such as Operations NEUTRALIZE and NIAGARA whereby the Air Commander is required to concentrate a major portion of his air effort in one area to preserve the posture of a friendly ground force. In other words, once the tactical situation at Khe Sanh reached the point that a sustained SLAM-type effort was required to provide primary defense, there was no question of the validity of the sustained requirement nor that the commitment would be honored. However, it is logical to assume that the enemy's choice of alternatives could allow him to plan for and take advantage of a situation such as the one created at Khe Sanh.

While stepping up infiltration into I Corps during the early part of NIAGARA operations, the enemy had also accelerated troop and supply movement through Laotian infiltration routes into the lower provinces of South Vietnam. Also, NVN and Pathet Lao hostilities against Royal Laotian forces and friendly Laotian villages and cities were on the rise -- especially along the eastern periphery of the NVN infiltration routes. It appeared that NVN strategy in this was not only to move friendly Laotian observers out of the area, but to widen his avenues of infiltration -- not only from Laos into South Vietnam, but through the highly motorable valley floors of Cambodia, for offensives in the lower Corps areas. Throughout NIAGARA, intelligence officials closely followed the enemy's reinforcement of his posture in the A Shau Valley, which was the target for Allied operations subsequent to NIAGARA. Enemy reaction had been much the same in the last part of 1967. While attention was focused on Operation NEUTRALIZE, they had begun moving their forces south for the Tet Offensive, which included Khe Sanh.

There has been much speculation about the enemy's real intentions in the Khe Sanh area. One position has been that Khe Sanh was a diversion for the Tet Offensive. An opposite estimate is that the widespread Tet Offensive was an attempt to dilute airpower availability in support of Khe Sanh. This was not accomplished; however, there was an impact on all out-of-country operations, except those considered to be essential. A MACV post-analysis concluded that all evidence indicated "conclusively" that the enemy had planned "a massive ground attack against the combat base supported by armor and artillery". The analysis stated that the enemy's initial target date apparently coincided with the Tet Offensive. Subsequent target dates estimated by MACV were:[198/]

- The last week in February. The enemy's heaviest attacks by fire at Khe Sanh occurred during the period 21-25 February.
- 13-14 March and 22-23 March. These dates were obtained through intelligence sources.

It is possible that Khe Sanh was just one of a few important objectives in an overall enemy attempt to win both a military and political victory, the difference being that its location made it more vulnerable than other targets. Whether it was a major or minor target, the fact remains that Khe Sanh was effectively pinned down and could have been overrun under the existing circumstances had it not been for airpower. If the enemy planned to launch a major assault against Khe Sanh, it is likely that NIAGARA Operations completely disrupted his timetable. A logical assumption would be that airpower and artillery had done more than destroy enemy forces and supplies; they had probably kept the enemy from effectively massing his forces for an assault. The enemy also undoubtedly suffered heavy losses in manpower and supplies from the NIAGARA air effort; however, with existing data, it is much too early to assess the final results.

Epilogue

By the end of March, it appeared that the enemy had abandoned any immediate thoughts of overrunning Khe Sanh. Reportedly, one of the divisions had been redeployed out of the area towards Hue.[199] COMUSMACV directed that Operation NIAGARA be terminated on 31 March,[200] with a follow-on joint effort known as Operation PEGASUS/LAMSON 207 to be executed on the same day to reopen the supply routes to Khe Sanh.[201]

Continued enemy presence in the area was clearly evident on the last day of NIAGARA operations when Khe Sanh received 347 incoming rounds over the 24 hour period. Six U.S. Marines were killed and twelve wounded. The area was quiet for two days, and then on 3 April the base received 152 rounds of mixed artillery and mortar fire resulting in five personnel wounded. By this time, Operation PEGASUS forces were sweeping in close to Khe Sanh, and in seven separate small unit contacts on 3 April ground forces killed 14 enemy. At 1735 hours on the 3rd, gunships from the A/1/9 Cav engaged an estimated 200 enemy in the open, and reported 20 enemy killed.[202]

On 4 April, elements of the 26th Marine Regiment secured Hill 471 to the south of Khe Sanh without enemy contact; however, artillery prep fires reportedly had killed 30 enemy soldiers on the hill. Also, after taking Hill 471, the Marines received approximately 120 rounds of mixed mortar, artillery, and rocket fire throughout the day. Seven Marines were killed and fifty were wounded, forty of whom were evacuated. Then, on 5 April at 0515 hours, Hill 471 received mortar and rocket fire followed by a ground attack from an estimated enemy battalion. After tactical air strikes and artillery were called in, the enemy broke contact at 0715 hours. Two U.S. Marines were wounded, 122 enemy were reported killed and three detained. Thirty-two individual weapons and 15 crew-served weapons were captured.[203/]

Other action continued throughout the area as friendly units moved out to secure other hills and landing zones and to reopen the supply routes. Many of the enemy were holed up in bunker complexes which required air strikes and artillery suppression in support of friendly sweeps. Several large ammunition and supply caches were discovered as friendly forces swept through the area around Khe Sanh. One situation was reported on 5 April which indicated poor battle discipline among the enemy ranks left behind. In the middle of the afternoon of the 5th, gunships from the 1/9 Cav observed 15 enemy in the open four kilometers southwest of Khe Sanh Village. The gunships engaged the enemy with machine guns and rockets, killing 15 enemy. In the same location ten minutes later, the gunships observed 35-40 enemy moving among the enemy dead from the previous attack.[204/]

The gunships attacked again, and 35 additional KIA were reported. Oddly, the enemy although well armed did not attempt to fire against the gunships. Gunship crews reported the battle area strewn with enemy dead and weaponry. Later, a sweep of the area disclosed 28 enemy KIA, and 12 individual weapons and one crew-served weapon. [205/]

On 12 April, Route 9 from Ca Lu to Khe Sanh was open to friendly traffic. In addition to reopening the Khe Sanh supply routes, one objective of Operation PEGASUS was to obtain additional information on results in NIAGARA. Much of the evidence was still being gathered, sifted, and reviewed by joint service teams. Khe Sanh appeared to be out of immediate danger, although enemy forces still held much of the high ground in the area. This high ground had been considerably altered. As one Marine officer commented: "The hills are numbered according to their height in meters above sea level. After NIAGARA, those numbers will have to be lowered." [206/]

MACV COC logs contained the following entries after 31 March which related specific air results in PEGASUS, or which could possibly be tied to the NIAGARA air effort: [207/]

- 5 April: At 1300 hours, 3 kilometers east of Khe Sanh, 1/5 Cav engaged an enemy force in a bunker complex. Organic weapons and friendly artillery, gunships and tactical air supporting. Estimated enemy 4 KIA; friendly 2 KIA.

- 5 April: At 1500 hours, 4 kilometers south of Khe Sanh, D/1/8 Cav engaged an enemy force in bunker complex. Both tactical air and artillery supported. Enemy broke contact. There were no friendly casualties; the enemy lost 11 KIA, one detained, two individual weapons and one crew-served weapon.

- 6 April: One kilometer east of Khe Sanh, the 37th Ranger Bn (ARVN), in a sweep of the area, found 70 enemy bodies which were credited to tactical air strikes and artillery. Numerous weapons were also captured.

- 6 April: One kilometer south of Khe Sanh, a USMC unit found six enemy dead with weapons.

- 9 April: One kilometer southeast of Khe Sanh Village, D/2/5 Cav found mass grave containing 35 bodies. (Could be enemy refugees)

- 7 April: Four kilometers northeast of Khe Sanh Village, an element of B/2/7 Cav found 24 enemy bodies, one individual weapon and one crew-served weapon.

- 8 April: Four kilometers west of Khe Sanh Village, at 0350 hours the 3rd ARVN CP was probed by an unknown size force. Air and Artillery supported. Results: Friendly 11 KIA, 20 WIA; Enemy 74 KIA, five detained, and 39 weapons captured.

- 9 April: One kilometer northwest of Khe Sanh Village, B/1/12 CAV found 59 enemy dead killed by tactical air strikes or artillery.

- 10 April: Nine kilometers southwest of Khe Sanh Village, A/1/9 Cav reported three tactical air strikes destroyed a tank and killed 15 enemy.

- 14 April: Eight kilometers northwest of Khe Sanh Base at 1428 hours, the 3rd Bn, 26th Marines secured Hill 881-N after extensive artillery and tactical air prep fires. Results: Friendly 6 KIA, 4 WIA; Enemy 106 KIA, 2 detained, and 66 weapons captured.

- 17 April: 2/3 USMC found bunkers and one cave containing a total of 16 enemy dead and three weapons.

Operation PEGASUS/LAMSON 207 was renamed Operation SCOTLAND II on 15 April. Cumulative results reported by MACV for PEGASUS/LAMSON 207 were as follows: Friendly 92 KIA (41 USA, 51 USMC), 667 WIA (208 USA, 459 USMC), 5 MIA (USA); Enemy 1,044 KIA, 9 detainees, 539 individual weapons and 184 crew-served weapons captured. [208/] 1,380 7AF, USN, and USMC tactical strike sorties and 210 B-52 sorties were flown in support of the operation. Cumulative results from the tactical air strikes were reported as follows: [209/]

- 68 secondary explosions and 43 secondary fires.
- 48 KBA.
- Five trucks and one tracked vehicle destroyed.
- 41 gun positions destroyed and seven damaged.
- 112 bunkers destroyed and 13 damaged.

FOOTNOTES

1. (S) Memorandum for Record, by Gen William W. Momyer, Comdr 7AF, subj: CIIB Meeting, 9 Jan 68 (Secret Material extracted from TS document); Memorandum by Gen William W. Momyer to Maj Gen Gordon F. Blood, 7AF, DCS Operations, subj: Air Support of I Corps, 21 Jan 68, Doc. 1; Memorandum for TACT Hq 7AF, by Brig Gen Jones E. Bolt, Dep Dir TACC Hq 7AF, subj: Niagara Operational Planning, 16 Jan 68.

2. (S) Statistical Data compiled by Hq 7AF DOSR for tactical air sorties and Hq MACV MACCOC8 for Arc Light sorties.

3. (S) Statistical Data made available by Hq 7AF DIP.

4. (S) Memorandum for Record, by Gen William W. Momyer, Comdr 7AF, subj: CIIB Meeting, 9 Jan 68. (Secret extract from Top Secret document)

5. (S) Msg, COMUSMACV to CINCPAC, subj: Operation Niagara, 151131Z Jan 68. (Secret extract from Top Secret document)

6. (S) Msg, Hq 7AF to Tiger Hound Addressees, subj: Operation Niagara, 20 Jan 68 (Secret extract from Top Secret document); Msg, COMUSMACV to CG III MAF, subj: Priority Arc Light Targeting, 6 Jan 68. (Secret extract from Top Secret document)

7. (S) Msg, COMUSMACV to CG III MAF, subj: Priority Arc Light Targeting, 6 Jan 68. (Secret extract from Top Secret document)

8. (S) Memorandum for Record, by Gen William W. Momyer, Comdr 7AF, subj: CIIB Meeting, 9 Jan 68. (Secret extract from Top Secret document)

9. Ibid.

10. (S) Memorandum by Comdr 7AF to DCS Operations 7AF, subj: Air Support of I Corps, 21 Jan 68. Doc. 1.

11. (S) Msg, COMUSMACV to Comdr 7AF, CG III MAF, CJCS, CINCPAC, CMC, CSAF, PACAF, FMFPAC, subj: Air Support of I Corps, 22 Jan 68.

12. (S) Msg, COMUSMACV to CINCPAC, subj: Air and Naval Support for I Corps, 22 Jan 68. (Secret extract from Top Secret document.)

13. (S) Msg, CINCPAC to COMUSMACV, subj: Naval Air Support for I Corps, 23 Jan 68. (Secret extract from Top Secret document.)

14. (S) Memorandum by Comdr 7AF to DCS Operations 7AF, subj: Air Support of I Corps, 21 Jan 68. Doc. 1.

15. (S) Msg, 7AF TACC to III MAF, subj: Operation Niagara, 19 Jan 68. (Secret extract from Top Secret document)

16. (S) Memorandum by Comdr 7AF to DCS Operations 7AF, subj: Air Support of I Corps, 21 Jan 68. Doc. 1.

17. (S) Msg, 7AF TACC to 504 TASC, 20th TASS, I DASC, and I Corps ALO, 22 Jan 68.

18. (S) Msg, Hq 7AF to Tiger Hound Addressees, subj: Operation Niagara, 20 Jan 68. (Secret extract from Top Secret document)

19. (S) Memorandum to Comdr 7AF, by Dep Dir TACC Hq 7AF, subj: Trip Report, 24 Jan 68. Doc. 2.

20. Ibid.

21. Ibid.

22. Ibid.

23. Ibid.

24. (S) Memorandum for ACofS, J-3, by Col Marcus L. Hill, Jr., USAF, MACCOC8, subj: Niagara Task Force Report, 9 Jan 68.

25. (C) MACV Combat Operations Center Log, 21-22 Jan 68.

26. (S) Msg, JANAF Attaches Vientiane Laos to DIA, subj: Situation Report, Laos, Debrief of Lt Col Soulang, CO, BV-33, 20 Feb 68, Doc. 3; Tigerhound/Tally Ho DISUMS, 23-24 Jan 68.

27. (S) Interview with Capt Charles Rushforth, and other Covey FACs, by Mr. Warren A. Trest, Hq 7AF Project CHECO, at Da Nang AB, 19 Feb 68. Docs. 4-8.

28. (S) Ibid; Hq 7AF DIS Logs.

29. (S) Msg, JANAF Attaches, Vientiane Laos to DIA, subj: Situation Report, Laos, Debrief of Lt Col Soulang, CO, BV-33, 20 Feb 68. Doc. 3.

30. (C) Interview with Capt Charles Rushforth, Covey FAC #252, 19 Feb 68. Doc. 4.

31. Ibid.

32. Ibid.

33. (S) Msg, JANAF Attaches Vientiane Laos to DIA, subj: Situation Report, Laos, Debrief of Lt Col Soulang, CO, BV-33, 20 Feb 68. Doc. 3.

34. Ibid.

35. (C) Interview with Covey FAC #252, 19 Feb 68. Doc. 4.

36. (C) Msg, AMEMB Vientiane to Sec State, subj: Situation Report, Laos, 21 Feb 68. Doc. 9.

37. (C) Msg, OLB 1, 6250th Spt Sq ABCCC to 7AF CC, subj: Hillsboro ABCCC Mission Report, 24 Jan 68.

38. (S) Msg, JANAF Attaches, Vientiane Laos to DIA, subj: Situation Report, Laos, Debrief of Lt Col Soulang, CO, BV-33, 20 Feb 68. Doc. 3.

39. (C) Interview with Covey FAC #252, 19 Feb 68. Doc. 4.

40. (C) Interview with Covey FAC #252, 19 Feb 68, and other Covey FACs, Docs. 4-8.

41. (SNF) Msg, COMUSMACV to AIG 7051, subj: J-2 MACV DISUM 23-68 for period 220001 to 222400 January, 23 Jan 68. Doc. 10.

42. (C) Msg, COMUSMACV to ZEN/NMCC, subj: Telecon, 24 Jan 68.

43. (C) TACC Duty Logs, 24 Jan 68.

44. (C) Interview with Covey FAC #252, 19 Feb 68. Doc. 4.

45. (SNF) Msg, COMUSMACV to AIG 7051, subj: J-2 MACV DISUM 23-68 for period 220001 to 222400 January, 23 Jan 68. Doc. 10.

46. (S) Memorandum for Record, by Comdr 7AF, subj: Employment of Forces, 24 Jan 68.

47. (S) Memorandum by Comdr 7AF to DCS Operations 7AF, subj: Tet and Niagara, 24 Jan 68.

48. (C) Sortie Statistical data compiled by Hq 7AF DOSR for tactical air sorties and Hq MACV for Arc Light sorties; BDA compiled by Hq 7AF DIS.

49. (C) Msg, COMUSMACV to VMAC, subj: Cancellation of Tet Offensive, 30 Jan 68.

50. (C) 7th Air Force TACC Logs, 29 Jan 68.

51. (C) Niagara Briefing, 7AF DIS, 1 Apr 68.

52. (S) Memorandum by Comdr 7AF to DCS/Operations 7AF, subj: Niagara, 30 Jan 68.

53. (C) Sortie Statistical Data compiled by Hq 7AF DOSR for tactical air sorties and Hq MACV for Arc Light sorties.

54. (C) Material provided by Hq 7AF DCS/Intelligence.

55. (S) Memorandum by Comdr 7AF to DCS/Operations 7AF, subj: Niagara, 2 Feb 68.

56. (S) Memorandum by Col H. H. Moreland, Hq 7AF TACP, subj: Diversion of In-Country Forces to Niagara, 2 Feb 68.

57. (S) Msg, Comdr 7AF to CG III MAF, CTF 77, subj: Niagara, 13 Feb 68.

58. (C) Statistical Data compiled by Hq 7AF DOSR for tactical air sorties and Hq MACV for Arc Light sorties.

59. (C) MACV COC Logs and DOSR 7AF Daily Reports on Sortie Rates.

60. (C) Hq 7AF DIS In-Country Intelligence Summary, 3-9 Feb 68.

61. (C) Interview with Covey FAC #232, Capt Gerald Herrington, at Da Nang AB, 19 Feb 68. Doc. 8.

62. (C) Hq 7AF DIS In-Country Intelligence Summary, 3-9 Feb 68; Hq MACV COC Log, 7 Feb 68.

63. (C) Interview with Covey FAC #232, 19 Feb 68. Doc. 8.

64. Ibid.

65. Ibid.

66. Ibid.

67. (C) Msg, OLB 1, 6250th Spt Sq ABCCC to 7AF CC, subj: Moonbeam ABCCC Mission Report, 7 Feb 68.

68. (C) Interview with Covey FAC #252, 19 Feb 68. Doc. 4.

69. Ibid.

70. Ibid.

71. Ibid.

72. (C) Msg, COMUSMACV to NMCC, subj: Special Telecon Khe Sanh/Lang Vei, 7 Feb 68. Doc. 11.

73. Ibid.

74. (C) Msg, OLB 1, 6250th Spt Sq ABCCC to 7AF TACC, subj: ABCCC JOPREP JIFFY, 7 Feb 68.

75. (C) MACV COC Log, 7 Feb 68.

76. (C) Interview with Covey FAC #232, 19 Feb 68. Doc. 8.

77. (C) Interview with Maj Milton G. Hartenbower, 7AF ALO to Khe Sanh, at Da Nang AB, 20 Feb 68. Doc. 6.

78. (S) Command Historical Chronology, 3rd Mar Div, Jan-Feb 68, on file at MACV History Office.

79. Ibid.

80. (C) Interview with Covey FACs, 19-20 Feb 68. Docs. 4-8.

81. (S) Command Historical Chronology, 3rd Marine Division, Jan-Feb 68.

82. (S) Msg, JANAF Attaches Vientiane, Laos to DIA, subj: Situation Report, Laos, Debrief of Lt Col Soulang, CO, BV-33, 20 Feb 68. Doc. 3.

83. Ibid.

84. (C) Interview with Covey FACs, 19-20 Feb 68. Docs. 4-8.

85. (C) Interview with Covey FAC #252, 19 Feb 68. Doc. 4.

86. Ibid.

87. Ibid.

88. (C) Msg, COMUSMACV to COMUSMACTHAI, subj: Weekly Review of Significant Intelligence as presented to COMUSMACV on 10 Feb 68, "Sphinx" 04262 by MACJ234.

89. (C) Hq 7AF DIS In-Country Intelligence Summary, 3-9 Feb 68.

90. (C) Interview with Covey FAC #252, 19 Feb 68. Doc. 4.

91. Ibid.

92. Ibid.

93. Ibid.

94. (C) Msg, OLB 1, 6250th Spt Sq, ABCCC, to Hq 7AF, subj: Hillsboro ABCCC Mission Report, 8 Feb 68.

95. (C) Interview with Covey FAC #252, 19 Feb 68. <u>Doc. 4</u>.

96. (C) Niagara briefing, by DCS/Intelligence.

97. (C) MACV COC Log, 23 Feb 68.

98. (C) Sortie rates documented by Hq 7AF DOSR.

99. (C) Niagara briefing, by DCS/Intelligence.

100. (S) Working Paper Message, on file DCS/Intelligence.

101. (S) Article prepared for Weekly Air Intelligence Summary, Hq 7AF, by Lt Col W. O. Ramey, Hq 7AF DIPA, 11 May 68.

102. (C) Material provided by Hq 7AF DCS/Intelligence.

103. <u>Ibid</u>.

104. <u>Ibid</u>.

105. <u>Ibid</u>.

106. <u>Ibid</u>.

107. <u>Ibid</u>.

108. <u>Ibid</u>.

109. (S) Article prepared for WAIS, Hq 7AF, by Lt Col W. O. Ramey, Hq 7AF DIPA, 11 May 68.

110. (C) Material provided by Hq 7AF DCS/Intelligence.

111. <u>Ibid</u>.

112. <u>Ibid</u>.

113. <u>Ibid</u>.

114. (S) Article prepared for WAIS, Hq 7AF, by Lt Col W. O. Ramey, Hq 7AF DIPA, 11 May 68.

115. <u>Ibid</u>.

116. (C) Tigerhound/Tally Ho DISUMS; ABCCC Mission Reports.

117. (S) Material provided by Hq 7AF DCS/Intelligence.

118. (C) ABCCC Mission Reports by OLB 1, 6250th Spt Sq, to Hq 7AF, 14-16 Feb 68.

119. Ibid.

120. Ibid.

121. Ibid.

122. (S) Article prepared for WAIS, Hq 7AF, by Lt Col W. O. Ramey, Hq 7AF DIPA.

123. (C) ABCCC Mission Reports by OLB 1, 6250th Spt Sq to Hq 7AF, 22 Jan-31 Mar 68.

124. Ibid.

125. (C) Interview with Covey FACs, Da Nang AB, 19 Feb 68. Docs. 4-8.

126. (C) Interview with Maj Milton G. Hartenbower, ALO to Khe Sanh, 19 Feb 68. Doc. 6.

127. (S) Msg, by Brig Gen Dale S. Sweat, Dir Combat Ops, Hq 7AF, to Niagara Tactical Air participants, subj: Close Air Support, 26 Feb 68.

128. (C) Msg, III MAF COC to MACV COC, subj: Niagara Daily Visual and Pad Surveillance Report, 27 Feb 68.

129. (S) Memorandum for Record by Col H. H. Moreland, Chief, Current Plans Division, TACC, subj: Response to Khe Sanh/Camp Carrol Crisis, 20 Feb 68.

130. (S) Msg, Dir Combat Ops Hq 7AF to Niagara Tactical Air Participants, subj: Close Air Support, 26 Feb 68.

131. (C) ABCCC Mission Report by OLB 1, 6250th Spt Sq to Hq 7AF, 25 Feb 68.

132. (C) Tigerhound/Tally Ho DISUM, 25 Feb 68.

133. (C) ABCCC Mission Report by OLB 1, 6250th Spt Sq to Hq 7AF, 24 Feb 68.

134. (C) ABCCC Mission Report by OLB 1, 6250th Spt Sq to Hq 7AF, 23 Feb 68.

135. (C) Tigerhound/Tally Ho DISUM, 24 Feb 68.

136. (C) Tigerhound/Tally Ho DISUM, 22 Feb 68.

137. (C) ABCCC Mission Report by OLB 1, 6250th Spt Sq to Hq 7AF, 24 Feb 68.

138. (C) Tigerhound/Tally Ho DISUM, 22 Feb 68.

139. Ibid.

140. Ibid.

141. (C) Interview with Covey #252, 19 Feb 68. Doc. 4.

142. (C) Interviews with FACs, 6 Jun 66-19 Feb 68.

143. (C) Tigerhound/Tally Ho DISUMS; Interviews with Covey FACs. Doc. 4-8.

144. (C) Tigerhound/Tally Ho DISUMS, 22-26 Feb 68.

145. (C) Ltr, Comdr 7AF to COMUSMACV, subj: Operation Niagara, undated. Doc. 12.

146. (S) Interview by 1st Lt Thomas Clark, Hq 7AF DIP, with Chief, MACCOC8, Hq MACV, 18 Apr 68.

147. (S) Msg, Hq SAC to CINCPAC, subj: Continuous Arc Light Emergency Capability for Operation Niagara, 101830Z Feb 68.

148. Ibid.

149. Ibid.

150. (S) Msg, CINCPAC to COMUSMACV, subj: Arc Light, 18 Feb 68.

151. (S) Msg, Hq SAC to CINCPAC, subj: Continuous Arc Light Emergency Capability for Operation Niagara, 101830Z Feb 68.

152. (S) Msg, COMUSMACV to CINCPAC, subj: Continuous Arc Light Emergency Capability for Operation Niagara, 13 Feb 68.

153. (S) End of Tour Report, Col Hilding L. Jacobson, Jr., Chief, SAC ADVON to Hq 7AF, to Comdr 7AF, 5 Apr 68; Msg, SAC to Amemb Vientiane, Laos, subj: Arc Light Overflight Summary Reports, 162200Z Feb 68.

154. (S) Msg, COMUSMACV to CINCPAC, subj: Arc Light, 130605Z Feb 68.

155. (S) Interview by 1st Lt Thomas Clark, Hq 7AF DIP, with Chief, MACCOC8, Hq MACV, 18 Apr 68.

156. (U) Ltr, Commanding Officer, 4th Marines, 3d Marine Division, FMF, APO 96602, Signed: William L. Dick (rank not listed), to Comdr 7AF, subj: Appreciation for Combat Support, 9 Feb 68.

157. (C) Material provided by Hq 7AF DCS/Intelligence.

158. Ibid.

159. Ibid.

160. Ibid.

161. (U) Airlift statistical data recorded by the Airlift Control Center, Tan Son Nhut AB.

162. (C) Interview with Covey FAC #251, Capt Joseph P. Johnson, at Da Nang AB, 20 Feb 68. Doc. 7.

163. (C) "History of Airlift at Khe Sanh," by 834th AD History Section.

164. Ibid.

165. Ibid.

166. (C) Interview with Maj Milton G. Hartenbower, 7AF ALO at Khe Sanh at Da Nang AB, 20 Feb 68. Doc. 6.

167. (C) Msg, CG III MAF to COMUSMACV, subj: Resupply of Khe Sanh, undated.

168. (C) Msg, CG III MAF to Comdr 7AF, subj: Khe Sanh Resupply, 26 Feb 68.

169. (C) Hq 7AF TACC logs; Mission Commander Reports, 834th AD; Interview by Capt Edward Vallentiny 7AF DOAC with Col William T. Phillips, Dir Airlift Command Center, 834th AD, 17 Apr 68.

170. (S) Msg, COMUSMACV to Comdr 7AF, CG III MAF, CJCS, CINCPAC, CMC, CSAF, PACAF, FMFPAC, subj: Air Support of I Corps, 22 Jan 68.

171. (S) Msg, CG III MAF to Comdr 7AF, subj: Air Support Control Operation Niagara, 240548Z Jan 68.

172. Ibid.

173. (C) Review of ABCCC Mission Reports and Tigerhound/Tally Ho DISUMS, 22 Jan-13 Feb 68; Docs. 13-50. Interviews with Covey FACs, and discussions with 7AF TACC officials.

174. Ibid.

175. Ibid.

176. Ibid.

177. Ibid.

178. Ibid.

179. Ibid.

180. (C) Msg, 7AF to Tiger Hound/Tally Ho Addressees, CG III MAF, CTG 77, and other Niagara participants, subj: Air Support in Defense of Khe Sanh, 13 Feb 68.

181. (S) Msg, CG III MAF to Comdr 7AF, subj: Air Effort for Defense of Khe Sanh, 140852Z Feb 68.

182. (C) ABCCC Mission Reports, Docs. 13-50.

183. Ibid.

184. (C) Msg, OLB 1 6250th Spt Sq ABCCC Udorn RTAFB Thai to 7AF, subj: Moonbeam ABCCC Mission Report, 160241Z Feb 68.

185. (C) "History of Airlift at Khe Sanh," by 834th AD History Section.

186. (U) Statistical Data sheet released by MACV on Khe Sanh, 11 Apr 68. Doc. 51.

187. (C) Hq 7AF TACC Logs, 15 Mar 68.

188. (C) ABCCC Mission Report by OLB 1, 6250th Spt Sq to Hq 7AF, 22 Mar 68.

189. (C) MACV COC Logs, 22-23 Mar 68.

190. (C) Sortie Statistical Data compiled by Hq 7AF DOSR for tactical air sorties and Hq MACV for Arc Light Sorties.

191. (C) ABCCC Mission Report by OLB 1, 6250th Spt Sq to Hq 7AF, 22 Mar 68.

192. (C) Sortie Statistical Data compiled by Hq 7AF DOSR for tactical air sorties and Hq MACV for Arc Light Sorties; BDA recorded daily by Hq 7AF DIS.

193. (C) Ibid; artillery data from MACV Fact Sheet. Doc. 51.

194. (C) BDA recorded daily by Hq 7AF DIS.

195. (C) Msg, COMUSMACV to DIA, subj: Effects of B-52 Strikes on VC/NVA Forces in the Khe Sanh Area, 201206Z Apr 68. Doc. 52.

196. Ibid.

197. Ibid.

198. (S) Memorandum for COMUSMACV, subj: An Analysis of the Khe Sanh Battle, by MACEVAL, 5 Apr 68. Doc. 53-68.

199. Ibid.

200. (S) Msg, COMUSMACV to CINCPAC, subj: Operation Niagara, 29 Mar 68.

201. (C) MACV COC Logs, 1 Apr 68.

202. (C) MACV COC Logs, 31 Mar - 3 Apr 68.

203. (C) MACV COC Logs, 4-5 Apr 68.

204. Ibid.

205. Ibid.

206. (C) MACV COC Log, 12 Apr 68; Interview by Lt Col W. O. Ramey, Hq 7AF DIPA with Marine officers at Dong Ha in Apr 68.

207 (C) MACV COC Logs, 1-17 Apr 68.

208. Ibid.

209. (C) Statistical Data by Hq 7AF DIS.

APPENDIX I

NIAGARA DAILY SORTIES*
23 Jan - 31 Mar

DATE	7AF	SAC	USN	USMC	TOTAL TAC
22 Jan	92	17	19	117	228
23 Jan	249	49	119	245	613
24 Jan	271	32	76	80	427
25 Jan	241	33	133	106	480
26 Jan	226	33	138	127	491
27 Jan	217	32	88	94	399
28 Jan	219	30	25	108	352
29 Jan	204	24	51	107	362
30 Jan	240	45	153	86	479
31 Jan	184	39	161	57	402
1 Feb	131	39	93	59	283
2 Feb	122	36	24	64	210
3 Feb	104	39	56	48	208
4 Feb	106	45	48	71	225
5 Feb	98	39	98	52	248
6 Feb	96	39	58	74	228
7 Feb	83	36	37	51	171
8 Feb	106	40	70	77	253
9 Feb	70	39	67	17	154
10 Feb	112	38	91	47	250
11 Feb	87	33	78	79	244

* Source: Hq 7AF TACC and Hq MACV

DATE	7AF	SAC	USN	USMC	TOTAL TAC
12 Feb	100	27	65	62	227
13 Feb	138	45	83	66	287
14 Feb	182	36	64	92	338
15 Feb	181	30	27	89	297
16 Feb	210	39	73	68	351
17 Feb	217	40	66	37	320
18 Feb	198	30	78	58	334
19 Feb	168	41	107	56	331
20 Feb	162	39	46	42	250
21 Feb	138	30	65	82	285
22 Feb	114	29	59	55	228
23 Feb	199	32	47	58	304
24 Feb	125	32	38	47	210
25 Feb	111	34	34	73	218
26 Feb	162	19	11	87	260
27 Feb	145	32	63	83	291
28 Feb	115	54	62	108	285
29 Feb	131	45	106	124	361
1 Mar	75	42	52	73	200
2 Mar	127	42	76	44	247
3 Mar	95	41	71	22	188
4 Mar	129	36	28	150	307
5 Mar	133	41	43	159	335
6 Mar	101	42	88	142	331

DATE	7AF	SAC	USN	USMC	TOTAL TAC
7 Mar	149	41	109	134	392
8 Mar	123	27	94	121	338
9 Mar	126	21	85	108	319
10 Mar	128	33	86	70	284
11 Mar	126	32	82	123	331
12 Mar	140	36	37	97	274
13 Mar	191	42	86	133	410
14 Mar	90	39	57	126	273
15 Mar	135	35	98	130	363
16 Mar	165	38	117	119	401
17 Mar	132	31	64	118	314
18 Mar	114	32	59	128	301
19 Mar	133	39	67	103	303
20 Mar	92	30	16	68	176
21 Mar	101	42	52	123	276
22 Mar	117	42	73	112	302
23 Mar	146	51	183	109	438
24 Mar	122	45	112	100	334
25 Mar	93	50	84	57	234
26 Mar	106	54	78	111	295
27 Mar	90	29	110	125	325
28 Mar	61	35	85	129	275
29 Mar	118	27	88	118	324
30 Mar	97	48	90	110	297
31 Mar	75	33	20	70	165

APPENDIX II

RECONNAISSANCE OBJECTIVES*
(PROGRESSIVE)

22 January - 29 January	Fragged	Successful
Black & White	627	282
Color	34	19
Camouflage Detection	39	21
Infra-red	345	115
High Acuity	27	5

22 January - 5 February		
Black & White	784	397
Color	54	32
Camouflage Detection	59	34
Infra-red	526	191
High Acuity	75	30

22 January - 12 February		
Black & White	940	424
Color	89	40
Camouflage Detection	95	41
Infra-red	83	29
High Acuity	142	30

* Source: Hq 7AF DIS

22 January - 19 February	Fragged	Successful
Black & White	1,169	486
Color	150	72
Camouflage Detection	176	76
Infra-red	805	239
High Acuity	205	30

22 January - 26 February	Fragged	Successful
Black & White	1,474	568
Color	185	83
Camouflage Detection	286	122
Infra-red	934	278
High Acuity	232	36

22 January - 4 March	Fragged	Successful
Black & White	1,796	647
Color	216	103
Camouflage Detection	332	137
Infra-red	1,010	312
High Acuity	250	36

22 January - 11 March	Fragged	Successful
Black & White	2,093	797
Color	236	113
Camouflage Detection	349	146
Infra-red	1,132	365
High Acuity	276	40

22 January - 18 March	Fragged	Successful
Black & White	2,334	907
Color	253	118
Camouflage Detection	370	154
Infra-red	1,219	388
High Acuity	309	67
22 January - 25 March		
Black & White	2,598	1,026
Color	253	118
Camouflage Detection	373	157
Infra-red	1,317	407
High Acuity	334	88
22 January - 31 March		
Black & White	2,839	1,122
Color	253	119
Camouflage Detection	385	162
Infra-red	1,389	444
High Acuity	345	79

APPENDIX III

TACTICAL AIR CUMULATIVE BDA*
(PROGRESSIVE)

22 January - 29 January	7AF	Navy/Marines
Secondary Explosions	149	56
Secondary Fires	106	35
Killed by Air	176	55
Trucks (Dest/Dam)	11/7	5/0
Gun Positions (Dest/Dam)	11/2	7/1
Bunkers (Dest/Dam)	11/0	18/10
Structures (Dest/Dam)	110/35	71/30

22 January - 5 February		
Secondary Explosions	269	119
Secondary Fires	326	103
Killed by Air	223	94
Trucks (Dest/Dam)	59/11	13/0
Gun Positions (Dest/Dam)	15/4	33/6
Bunkers (Dest/Dam)	34/2	180/11
Structures (Dest/Dam)	181/35	149/30

* Source: Hq 7AF DIS (Collected as of 31 March through visual sightings only)

22 January - 12 February	7AF	Navy/Marines
Secondary Explosions	327	156
Secondary Fires	367	205
Killed by Air	284	218
Trucks (Dest/Dam)	62/11	17/2
Gun Positions (Dest/Dam)	18/4	39/6
Bunkers (Dest/Dam)	43/4	202/11
Structures (Dest/Dam)	303/38	336/54
Tanks (Dest/Dam)	3/0	2/3

22 January - 19 February		
Secondary Explosions	1277	397
Secondary Fires	396	252
Killed by Air	304	240
Trucks (Dest/Dam)	66/13	20/5
Gun Positions (Dest/Dam)	33/7	48/6
Bunkers (Dest/Dam)	44/4	243/12
Structures (Dest/Dam)	328/38	371/54
Tanks (Dest/Dam)	4/0	2/3

22 January - 26 February		
Secondary Explosions	1321	422
Secondary Fires	434	285
Killed by Air	339	256
Trucks (Dest/Dam)	78/14	22/7
Gun Positions (Dest/Dam)	44/12	51/8
Bunkers (Dest/Dam)	57/4	251/12

	7AF	Navy/Marines
Structures (Dest/Dam)	332/38	381/84
Tanks (Dest/Dam)	4/0	3/3

22 January - 4 March

	7AF	Navy/Marines
Secondary Explosions	1461	464
Secondary Fires	546	329
Killed by Air	417	285
Trucks (Dest/Dam)	89/15	26/8
Gun Positions (Dest/Dam)	54/12	54/8
Bunkers (Dest/Dam)	73/6	258/12
Structures (Dest/Dam)	406/43	394/84
Tanks (Dest/Dam)	4/0	4/4

22 January - 11 March

	7AF	Navy/Marines
Secondary Explosions	1651	687
Secondary Fires	703	415
Killed by Air	490	399
Trucks (Dest/Dam)	102/18	36/10
Gun Positions (Dest/Dam)	74/13	79/15
Bunkers (Dest/Dam)	98/8	373/32
Structures (Dest/Dam)	419/45	459/96
Tanks (Dest/Dam)	4/0	4/4

22 January - 18 March	7AF	Navy/Marines
Secondary Explosions	1795	770
Secondary Fires	1019	519
Killed by Air	570	468
Trucks (Dest/Dam)	93/15	92/17
Gun Positions (Dest/Dam)	151/27	38/11
Bunkers (Dest/Dam)	122/9	449/32
Structures (Dest/Dam)	524/45	481/96
Tanks (Dest/Dam)	4/0	5/4

22 January - 25 March		
Secondary Explosions	2179	1040
Secondary Fires	1116	593
Killed by Air	641	566
Trucks (Dest/Dam)	164/33	44/14
Gun Positions (Dest/Dam)	135/18	144/21
Bunkers (Dest/Dam)	153/12	563/79
Structures (Dest/Dam)	563/51	487/100
Tanks (Dest/Dam)	4/0	5/4

22 January - 31 March		
Secondary Explosions	2215	1128
Secondary Fires	1173	651

	7AF	Navy/Marines
Killed by Air	650	638
Trucks (Dest/Dam)	204/37	49/15
Gun Positions (Dest/Dam)	135/18	165/25
Bunkers (Dest/Dam)	216/19	675/80
Structures (Dest/Dam)	564/52	497/106
Tanks (Dest/Dam)	4/0	5/4

APPENDIX IV

PHOTO SIGNIFICANT ITEMS* (PROGRESSIVE)

	29 Jan	5 Feb	12 Feb	19 Feb	26 Feb	4 Mar	11 Mar	18 Mar	25 Mar	31 Mar
Bunkers	173	180	190	243	258	258	262	282	292	301
Trenches	4	5	5	55	56	59	64	65	65	72
Strong Points	12	23	50	52	78	78	78	84	85	86
Gun Positions	101	144	143	151	172	180	211	230	236	238
POL Drums	136	136	136	136	136	136	136	151	151	151
Foxholes	576	636	661	661	1,042	1,254	1,544	1,544	1,544	1,544
Mortar Positions	23	31	31	36	36	55	55	66	80	80
Tanks	0	4	5	5	5	5	5	5	5	5
Troops	93	93	128	130	147	147	147	147	147	147

TARGET STATUS 22 Jan – 31 Mar

	Targets Nominated	Targets Fragged	Struck	Deleted	Active
Logistics	318	490	169	261	57
LOCs	84	74	19	81	3
Truck Parks	55	60	15	20	35
Weapons	566	663	291	389	177
Troops	547	617	253	420	127
Control/Comm	46	61	24	31	15
Fortifications	427	414	205	230	197
Miscellaneous	4	2	2	3	1

* Source: Hq 7AF DIS

APPENDIX V

TOTAL ORDNANCE EXPENDED
by 7th AIR FORCE

AMMO	FIRE BOMB	FLARES	ANTI-MAT	INC-CLUST	ANTI-PERS
744,000	1,263	576	315	500	579

FRAG-CLUST	INC-SMOKE	ROCKET	SPIKE	GLVB-30	250	500
64	118	1,390	8	36	794	21,621

750	1000	2000	3000	BULL-PUP
15,362	120	33	30	20

APPENDIX VI

KHE SANH AIRLIFT SUMMARY

DATE	LAND	TONS	CDS LAPES	TONS	LAND	TONS	DROP	TONS	TOTAL SORTIES	TOTAL TONS
JAN										
21					6	25.8			6	25.8
22					20	88.2			20	88.2
23	14	174.4							14	174.4
24	18	253.2			1	.3			19	253.5
25	13	156.9	4	55.0	1	1.4			18	213.3
26	13	225.3			1	.5			*16	*227.1
27	23	312.2			1	.4			*27	*318.7
28	8	111.0	1	12.0	2	9.4			*14	*126.0
29	24	289.7							24	289.7
30	18	250.7			2	3.5			20	254.2
31	24	288.9			6	25.5			30	314.4
FEB										
1	16	221.7			2	3.4			18	225.1
2	2	23.4			1	4.8			3	28.2
3	1	14.2							1	14.2
4	11	160.6							11	160.6
5	15	202.9			2	7.1			17	210.0
6	11	148.5							11	148.5
7	10	144.1			1	4.9			11	149.0
8	20	245.9			1	4.1			21	250.0

Source: 834th AD ALCC

DATE FEB	LAND	TONS	CDS	LAPES	TONS	LAND	TONS	DROP	TONS	TOTAL SORTIES	TOTAL TONS
9	3	27.0				1	5.0			4	32.0
10	6	45.0								6	45.0
11	9	101.1								9	101.1
12						7	41.3			7	41.3
13			2		30.0	11	32.7			13	62.7
14			7		98.0	18	102.0			25	200.0
15			5		75.0	11	46.0			16	121.0
16			8	4	149.0	6	19.9			18	168.9
17			8		122.6					8	122.6
18			10		156.1					10	156.1
19			7	2	122.8					9	122.8
20			9		169.3	1	5.0			**10	**174.3

* Includes C-7As

** Totals include 8 C-7A sorties (13 tons)

KHE SANH AIRLIFT SUMMARY

DATE	C-130 LAND	C-130 TONS	C-130 CDS	C-130 LAPES	C-130 TONS	C-123 LAND	C-123 TONS	C-123 DROP	C-123 TONS	TOTAL SORTIES	TOTAL TONS
FEB											
21			10	4	183.4	1	4.9			15	188.3
22			10		143.3	2	10.6			12	153.9
23			10		156.2	2	8.3			12	164.5
24			9		117.1	5	20.7			14	137.8
25			9		141.7	2	8.0	1	3.0	12	152.7
26	1	8.5	9	2	149.7	3	12.5	1	3.1	16	173.8
27	3	38.0	10	1	152.5	4	12.7			18	203.2
28	5	51.4	9		149.9	1	4.8			15	206.1
29	5	62.7	10		152.8	6	22.7	1	1.8	22	240.0
MAR											
1			5	1	79.9	7	32.8			13	112.7
2			10	2	169.8	1	4.0	1	3.2	14	177.0
3			10		152.2	1	1.9	1	1.8	12	155.7
4			10		151.1	3	14.0	3	7.5	16	172.6
5			10		138.1	2	7.3	2	7.8	14	153.2
6			8		121.3	5	20.6	3	9.5	16	151.4
7			10		150.6			1	1.4	11	152.0
8			10		151.0			2	3.6	12	154.6
9			7	3	128.2	3	15.1			11	143.3
10			11	1	167.1	1	1.2	3	8.0	16	176.3
11			11		164.3	2	6.7	2	7.4	15	178.4
12			10	2	157.3			2	4.0	12	161.3

	C-130					C-123					
DATE	LAND	TONS	CDS	LAPES	TONS	LAND	TONS	DROP	TONS	TOTAL SORTIES	TOTAL TONS
MAR											
13			12	2	194.9			4	10.7	18	205.6
14			9		134.7			4	8.6	13	143.3
15			12		171.2	1	4.6	3	9.2	16	185.0
16			14	1	211.2	4	10.2	2	16.0	21	237.4
17			13		206.8	2	8.4	3	12.8	19	228.0
18			14	5	245.8	1	4.6	3	9.8	23	260.2
19			15	1	216.8	1	4.2	2	6.4	19	227.4
20			13	1	190.8	1	4.8	4	7.9	19	203.5
21			10	1	142.3			5	15.5	16	157.8
22			11	1	164.5	2	6.8	4	10.2	18	181.5
23			10	2	152.8	1	3.9	4	10.6	17	167.3
24			10	1	157.1	1	4.0	4	8.9	16	170.0
25			10	1	151.3					11	151.3
26			9	2	139.0			2	4.9	13	143.9
27			7		100.2	1	5.4	2	6.3	10	111.9
28			10	1	151.5			4	11.9	15	163.4
29			10	2	154.3	1	4.0	2	4.5	15	162.8
30	(1 GPES)		4	2	71.7	2	8.5	2	4.1	11	84.3
31			6	4	95.8	1	1.1	4	12.6	15	109.5
APR											
1	(1 GPES)		5	1	106.4	1	3.6	4	13.0	13	123.0
2			5	2	85.3			4	9.1	11	94.4
3			5		76.4			3	7.4	8	83.8

	C-130					C-123				TOTAL	TOTAL
DATE	LAND	TONS	CDS	LAPES	TONS	LAND	TONS	DROP	TONS	SORTIES	TONS
APR											
4		(3 GPES)		5	100.0	1	5.3	4	5.9	13	111.2
5		(3 GPES)		5	95.8	1	5.5	1	2.1	10	103.4
6		(4 GPES)		5	109.7	2	5.6			11	115.3
7		(3 GPES)		5	104.8			4	12.9	12	117.7
8				2	27.4	2	8.4	4	11.0	6	46.8
TOTAL:	273	3557.8	496	52	7825.8	179	738.9	105	294.3	*1124	*12430.0
		3558	(GPES 15)		7826		739		294		12430

GPES = Ground Proximity Extraction System

CDS = Container Delivery System

LAPES = Low Altitude Parachute Extraction System

* Totals Include Eight (8) C-7A Sorties (13 Tons)

AIRDROPS		AIRLAND	
C-130	7826	C-130	3558.0
C-123	294	C-123	739.0
		C-7A	13.0
TOTAL	8120	TOTAL	4310

GLOSSARY

AA	Antiaircraft
AAA	Antiaircraft Artillery
AB	Air Base
ABCCC	Airborne Command and Control Center
AD	Air Division
ADVON	Advanced Echelon
AF	Air Force
AGL	Above Ground Level
ALCC	Airlift Control Center
ALO	Air Liaison Officer
AO	Air Observer
AP	Armor Piercing
APC	Armored Personnel Carrier
ARVN	Army of the Republic of Vietnam
AW	Automatic Weapon
BDA	Bomb Damage Assessment
CAP	Combat Air Patrol
CAS	Close Air Support
CBU	Cluster Bomb Unit
CDS	Container Delivery System
CG	Commanding General
CIDG	Civilian Irregular Defense Group
CINCPAC	Commander in Chief, Pacific
CO	Commanding Officer
COC	Combat Operations Center
COMUSMACV	Commander U.S. Military Assistance Command, Vietnam
CONUS	Continental United States
CP	Command Post
CSS	COMBAT SKYSPOT
CTZ	Corps Tactical Zone
DASC	Direct Air Support Center
DI	Director of Intelligence
DMZ	Demilitarized Zone
FAC	Forward Air Controller
FSCC	Fire Support Control Center
GCA	Ground-Controlled Approach
GPES	Ground Proximity Extraction System
HUMINT	Human Intelligence

ICC	Intelligence Control Center
IDHS	Intelligence Data Handling System
IP	Initial Point
JCS	Joint Chiefs of Staff
KBA	Killed by Air
KIA	Killed in Action
LAPES	Low Altitude Parachute Extraction System
LOC	Lines of Communication
LZ	Landing Zone
MACV	Military Assistance Command, Vietnam
MAF	Marine Amphibious Force
MAW	Marine Air Wing
MIA	Missing in Action
NCO	Noncommissioned Officer
NVA	North Vietnamese Army
NVN	North Vietnam
NW	Northwest
OIC	Officer in Charge
PI	Photo Interpreter
POL	Petroleum, Oil, Lubricants
POW	Prisoner of War
SA	Small Arms
SAC	Strategic Air Command
SAM	Surface to Air Missile
SE	Southeast
SF	Special Forces
SLAM	Seek, Locate, Annihilate, and Monitor
SSE	South Southeast
SSW	South Southwest
STOL	Short Take Off and Landing
SVN	South Vietnam
TACC	Tactical Air Control Center
TACP	Tactical Air Control Party
TACS	Tactical Air Control System
TAOR	Tactical Area of Operational Responsibility
TASS	Tactical Air Support Squadron
TDY	Temporary Duty
TOC	Tactical Operations Center
TOT	Time Over Target

USA	United States Army
USAF	United States Air Force
USMC	United States Marine Corps
USN	United States Navy
USSF	United States Special Forces
VC	Viet Cong
VR	Visual Reconnaissance
WAAPM	Wide Area Anti-personnel Mine
WAIS	Weekly Air Intelligence Summary
WIA	Wounded in Action

PACAF - HAFB, Hawaii

www.ingramcontent.com/pod-product-compliance
Lightning Source LLC
Chambersburg PA
CBHW080546170426
43195CB00016B/2696